Theda Bara, My Mentor

Theda Bara, My Mentor

Under the Wing of Hollywood's First Femme Fatale

JOAN CRAIG
with BEVERLY F. STOUT

McFarland & Company, Inc., Publishers
Jefferson, North Carolina

LIBRARY OF CONGRESS CATALOGUING DATA ARE AVAILABLE

Names: Craig, Joan, 1941– author. | Stout, Beverly F., author.
Title: Theda Bara, my mentor : under the wing of Hollywood's first femme fatale / Joan Craig with Beverly F. Stout.
Description: Jefferson, North Carolina : McFarland & Company, Inc., Publishers, 2016 | Includes index.
Identifiers: LCCN 2016009417 | ISBN 9781476662831 (softcover : acid free paper) ∞
Subjects: LCSH: Bara, Theda, 1890–1955—Friends and associates. | Craig, Joan, 1941–
Classification: LCC PN2287.B178 C73 2016 | DDC 791.4302/8092—dc23
LC record available at https://lccn.loc.gov/2016009417

BRITISH LIBRARY CATALOGUING DATA ARE AVAILABLE

**ISBN (print) 978-1-4766-6283-1
ISBN (ebook) 978-1-4766-2287-3**

© 2016 Joan Craig with Beverly F. Stout. All rights reserved

No part of this book may be reproduced or transmitted in any form or by any means, electronic or mechanical, including photocopying or recording, or by any information storage and retrieval system, without permission in writing from the publisher.

Front cover photograph of Theda Bara, Hoover Art Company, Los Angeles (The Stout Collection)

Printed in the United States of America

McFarland & Company, Inc., Publishers
Box 611, Jefferson, North Carolina 28640
www.mcfarlandpub.com

This book is dedicated to
my daughter, grandchild, and to you,
the reader, for your enjoyment.

Table of Contents

Acknowledgments xi
Preface 1

1. Theda, the Early Years
Future Woman 5 | Omens of Luck 13

2. Joan, the Early Years
California, Land of Dreams 17

3. First Meeting
The Lady in the House 21 | Magical Move and Spirits 27

4. Settling In
The Brown Derby	30	Mansion on West Adams	42
Flying Tigers	30	Edendale and Cleopatra	45
The Afterlife	32	Theda Shops at Home	46
Open House	36	The Brabins, Mae, and Sid	46
A Croquet Garden Party	38	Invite a Friend	48
The Shadow of the Sphinx	38	Audition	50

5. Remembering
Fortune	51	A Crashed Flying Disc	63
Gable, Fleming and Bergman	51	Finishing the Script	64
Bergman as Joan of Arc	56	September	66
A Masquerade Party	57	Joan of Arc at the Stake	66
Easter in Beverly Hills Hotel	58	A Television Party	67
Communism in Hollywood	59	158th Infantry Regiment	68
A Night to Remember	61		

6. Friends for Life

1948	69	Finding Montgomery Clift	78
Marionettes	69	The Pageant of the Masters	81
The Metropolitan Opera	70	Theda's Life Story	81
Adoption	71	On Location with *Cleopatra*	82
Canasta	73	Contract Signed	85
The Premiere of *Joan of Arc*	75	Stock Market on the Rise	85
Hollywood Loses Fleming	76	Ambassador to Luxembourg	87
You Have the Best Part	76		

7. Traveling Abroad

The Coronation	89	Kissing the Blarney Stone	96
St. Donat's Castle, Wales	92		

8. Back Home in Los Angeles

The Disney Dream	98	The Last Party	103
At Home	100		

9. My Theda

Be True to Yourself	105	The Following Years	106

10. The Stage Plays

1908: *The Devil*	109	1920: *The Blue Flame*	111
1912: *The Quaker Girl*	110		

11. The Films

1914: *The Stain*	114	*Gold and the Woman*	127
A Fool There Was	114	THEDA TALKS TO THE PUBLIC	128
1915: *The Kreutzer Sonata*	118	*The Eternal Sapho*	131
The Clemenceau Case	118	*East Lynne*	132
The Devil's Daughter	120	*Under Two Flags*	134
Lady Audley's Secret	121	*Her Double Life*	134
The Two Orphans	121	*Romeo and Juliet*	135
Sin	122	*The Vixen*	137
Carmen	123	1917: *The Darling of Paris*	138
The Galley Slave	125	*The Tiger Woman*	140
Destruction	125	*Her Greatest Love*	141
1916: *The Serpent*	125	*Heart and Soul*	141

Camille 142	1919: *The Light* 156
Cleopatra 143	*When Men Desire* 158
The Rose of Blood 147	*The Siren's Song* 160
Du Barry 147	*A Woman There Was* 162
1918: *The Forbidden Path* 148	*Kathleen Mavourneen* 162
The Soul of Buddha 150	*La Belle Russe* 166
Under the Yoke 152	*The Lure of Ambition* 167
Salome 152	1925: *The Unchastened*
When a Woman Sins 153	*Woman* 168
The She-Devil 154	1926: *Madame Mystery* 168

12. Charles Brabin

Uncle Charlie and Me 171	Brabin Filmography 189
The Early Years 177	

Index 201

Acknowledgments

I would like to thank so many wonderful people who helped or inspired me in the preparation of this book.

I express my gratitude to Beverly Stout who saw me through the book. She provided encouraging support while I relived my childhood. She has provided the most interesting collection of photographs and assisted in the editing, proofreading and design.

I would like to thank the following people who gave me the incentive and courage to write about my neighbors, Theda and Charles, who devotedly gave me an education and a special introduction to the art of imagination: Mathew Brabin Bessell; Robert S. Birchard, film editor, author and film historian; Peter Brabin Bridgstock; Helena C. Carta; the Clarke Historical Museum; Ronald Genini, film historian and author of *Theda Bara: A Biography;* Eve Golden, author of *Vamp: The Rise and Fall of Theda Bara*; Andi Hicks, producer, editor and writer at Timeline Films; Cathryn MacEllerhan; Hugh Munro Neely, documentarian, producer, director, and founder of Timeline Films and producer of *The Woman with the Hungry Eyes*, Marilyn Slater, author and Mabel Normand historian; and Jerry Wallace.

I would also like to thank Matthew Lutts, sales executive, and Glenn White, customer support, of the Associated Press Images; Faye Thompson, photographic archive coordinator, and Janet Lorenz, NFIS researcher, of the Academy of Motion Pictures, Arts and Sciences (Margaret Herrick Library); Hap Byers, photographer; Lynne Crandall, owner of Décor Art Galleries, Inc.; Peter Okicich, secretary-treasurer of Flying Tiger Line Pilots Association; Andy Howick of mptv images; Thomas Lisanti, manager, Permissions & Reproduction Services, New York Public Library; Wayne Shoaf of the University of Southern California Libraries, Special Collections; Yuri Shcherbina, metadata manager of the University of

California Libraries; Dace Taube, head of Special Collections, the University of Southern California; Bruce Calvert of the Silent Film Still Archive (website); Tim Lussier of Silents Are Golden (website); the late Polish painter Eliasz Kanarek (for the Joan Craig painting); Joyce Glenna Holaday, for her knowledge and guidance regarding early and golden age cinema.—Joan Craig

Preface

I first met Joan Craig through her dealings with Heritage Auctions. She had put up for auction several costumes and accessories worn by Theda Bara in some of her most iconic films. Shortly before Theda passed away on April 7, 1955, she had become aware that her illness was terminal and she chose to leave her cherished costumes to her young friend, Joan.

Joan and Theda had become good friends over the years before Theda's death. Theda and Charles Brabin had no children of their own, and upon meeting little Joan, both of the Brabins embraced her as family. She truly became a part of the Brabin household, often visiting Theda and Charles after school and during the summer. Likewise, little Joan became enchanted by these two amazing people. Both Theda and Charles spent time with Joan, teaching her how to maneuver through life and instructing her in such varied subjects as history, languages, religions, the film industry, etiquette and so much more. Joan Craig's parents were friends with the Brabins and knew that their daughter was in good hands in the Brabin household. Many times Theda would have cookies or sandwiches prepared for Joan when she came over to visit.

During the auction, I began to correspond with Joan regarding the items up for auction. In the course of our conversation, Joan mentioned that she wanted to write a book about her life with Theda. As I listened to her stories, I became amazed at the information about Joan's early life with Theda and Charles. I knew that Joan's story needed to be told. I had already read the two biographies written on the life of Theda Bara. The Eve Golden biography, *Vamp: The Rise and Fall of Theda Bara,* was published in 1996 by Emprise Publishing, Inc., and *Theda Bara: A Biography,* was written by the film historian Ronald

Genini, and also published that same year by McFarland. Both biographies are excellent and I can appreciate the time and detailed work both authors put into them. Joan and I recommend these books as definitive biographies on the life and work of Theda Bara. Ms. Golden and Mr. Genini present us with the facts of Theda's life and give us a glimpse into the person Theda was by her actions and her words, photographs, and the recollections of others. Other information has been gathered on Theda's life in various written, recorded, and photographic formats.

However, after listening to the stories that Joan told me, I began to truly understand who these two people were. Having worked in book design, publishing, photography and photographic restoration, I felt that I could help Joan realize the dream of getting her book presented to the public. Seven years ago our project was born. We became friends, which was quite amazing since I am a Mississippian by birth, born and raised in the cotton fields of the Mississippi Delta, and Joan was raised in the star-studded city of Los Angeles. However, we had one thing in common: an appreciation for the life and work of Theda Bara and in Joan's case, a true love and affection for her friend, the star the public knows as the first great Vamp of silent film.

Theda Bara as Salome, from the film *Salome*, 1918 (Stout Collection).

Our memory of Theda Bara has survived the passage of time; however, her films have not. For instance, Julian Fellowes, the highly esteemed writer-producer of TV's *Downton Abbey*, made reference to Theda in his dialogue for Season Two, Episode Seven. Carson, the head butler, states: "Oh, you should see some of the gadgets in the kitchens.

And the bathrooms, oh, goodness me. They're like something out of a film with Theda Bara." No doubt Mr. Fellowes was referencing the huge, elaborate old Victorian set pieces and fancy decorations which were used in Theda's movies.

It is fairly easy to see movies starring Mary Pickford or Charlie Chaplin; however, it is not possible to find copies of Theda's best movies. On July 9, 1937, the Little Ferry, New Jersey, vault where Fox Film Corporation stored their silent films burned to the ground. The old nitrate films must have fueled the fire tremendously. Of Theda's 44 films, only four complete films are known to exist as of this writing. Her first starring film, A *Fool There Was*, exists, as does *East Lynne*, *The Unchastened Woman*, as well as *Madame Mystery*, her last short film, produced by Hal Roach.

In 2006, Timeline Films produced a documentary on the life of Theda Bara entitled *The Woman with the Hungry Eyes*. Hugh Munro Neely directed and narrated the film and Dana Delany provided the voice of Theda Bara. The film is superbly produced and I am quite amazed that Mr. Neely was able to find such elusive information on the star. It puts one more piece in the puzzle and helps us understand who Theda Bara was, and Joan and I both highly recommend the film.

Joan Craig has given us a real treasure with her memoir, *Theda Bara, My Mentor: Under the Wing of Hollywood's First Femme Fatale*. The elusive Theda Bara (born simply Theodosia Burr Goodman in Cincinnati, Ohio) becomes a real person and, as all will come to understand, a very intelligent and highly driven person. But most of all, Theda was a caring person. It is this caring that encompassed little Joan Craig. Theda truly loved Joan and cared very much about her future. Joan, with the publication of her memoir, returns the love and comes full circle with her life.

In the book, Joan presents her early life and time spent with her friend. In the second half of the book, we have included both stills and lobby cards from most of Theda's films. Joan felt it of the utmost importance for the public to become familiar with Theda's films and she includes a short synopsis of each movie. In keeping with that theme, we include the names of the characters Theda played in those films. I have attempted to identify stills by their production number so that we might have more information about these lost movies. We feel that it is imperative that we identify as many of Theda's film stills as possible, as well as other stills from the silent era.

Before I close, I would like to impart to the reader what I have learned about Theda Bara over the years. People ask what was she like. I did not know Theda as Joan did, but I have learned so much about her. These are my impressions: She was indeed, a fine person. She was very educated, via her college attendance, her family life and her family history. She was extremely talented, and also multi-talented; she played piano and could speak several languages. She seemed to be born an actor, having started at such an early age, and by all descriptions of her at this age, she seems to have loved the craft. It came so naturally to her. She took that craft very seriously, right down to small details like having the proper period costumes. She learned as much as she could about the characters she played in preparation for her roles. She was also a family-oriented person, and loyal to the people she loved. She truly cared about her public and she worried over how she was perceived due to the characters she portrayed. Theda was not perfect by any means. It has been reported that she was hard to work with and that mishaps occasionally happened in filming certain scenes. However, I believe that one must be somewhat temperamental to succeed in the art of acting. It is not an easy job.

Even though Theda was portrayed as a Vamp, she was quite the opposite in real life. I will also address the issue of some of Theda's scantily clad characters. After seeing many of Theda's stills, I think that she drew the line regarding nudity in her films. She would portray the character as she thought the character dressed, but only up to her limit. Cleopatra in her snake bra is quite revealing, however; that seems to be as far as Theda would go. I believe that setting the limit was her way of dealing with those problems of the day. For Theda, it was all about the film and getting the character portrayed as accurately as possible. Theda Bara was truly a unique individual. As you read about her, you will become inspired.

I would like to take this opportunity to thank Joan Craig for placing her trust in me to help her with this project. For Joan and I both, thanks go to Theda and Charles Brabin. It is truly Theda, through her work in films and the great person whom she was, who ultimately inspired us to complete this important project. We sincerely hope you enjoy it. As I close, I am truly in wonder at the friendship between Theda and little Joan Craig. It can best be summed up as a loving friendship that will last throughout the ages.—Beverly Stout

1

Theda, the Early Years

Future Woman

Theda Bara's mother, Pauline Louise de Coppet Baranger (1861–1957), was born to French parents, François Baranger and Régine (de Rininger) de Coppet, in La Chaux-de-Fonds, Switzerland. Pauline Louise and her brother were orphaned after the death of their parents, who died young. The children were eventually brought to America by their uncle, who had been a court surgeon to the first Emperor of the Austrian and Austro-Hungarian Monarchy. Soon after their arrival, Pauline and her brother were scammed out of their inheritance. Pauline Louise's brother got into a fight with the swindler and was blamed. He was arrested and shortly after died in prison.

Theda's father, Bernard Goodman (1853–1936), arrived at Ellis Island in 1871 from Chorzele, Poland. The name Goodman was not the original family surname; it was thought to be assigned due to a mix-up while being processed through Ellis Island. Bernard's original surname was Gutterman, but because he had been assigned Goodman in his new country, he decided it best to keep it.

Settling in Cincinnati, Ohio, Goodman was employed as a foreman cutter at a tailor shop in Avondale, Ohio. He would often pass by Dunkelmyer and de Coppet, Wig Makers, while en route to and from work. There he met Pauline, an employee, and soon attempted to court her. She often rebuffed his attentions. One day in 1882, Bernard, undeterred, arrived at her shop with roses in hand and proposed marriage to her in French. Impressed by his tenacity, she finally accepted and they were married the next day. After a period of time, Bernard became a men's clothing designer and a partner in Ochs, Weihl, and Goodman, Tailors.

Theda was born on July 29, 1885. Pauline Louise named her first-

Theda Bara. Underwood and Underwood Studios, New York, c. 1919 (Stout Collection).

born child after Aaron Burr's daughter, Theodosia Burr. Burr recognized the rights of women and wanted his daughter's education to be not only equal to, but superior to men's. His daughter Theodosia was to be a woman of the future.

Theda was raised in a traditional Jewish home environment, the

1. Theda, the Early Years

one exception being that her mother spoke only Francoprovencal. In addition to learning English, the Goodman children also learned to speak Russian, Polish, Lithuanian and Italian.

After living in several residences in Cincinnati, Theda's family set-

Theda poses with the flag (ca. 1888) at about the age of three. Already she had learned the importance of posing for the camera (Billy Rose Theater Division, The New York Library for the Performing Arts, Astor, Lenox and Tilden Foundations).

tled in the wealthy community of Avondale, which showcased large Victorian-styled homes. The Goodman house had a carriage stone in front marked GOODMAN. Even though Avondale was within minutes of downtown Cincinnati, it also had its own neighborhood shopping district. Theda—or Teddy, as she became known—was the eldest of three children. Theda's brother was Marque "Buddy" Goodman (1888–1954) and her sister was Esther "Lori" Goodman, (1897–1965).

In spite of preventive door locks and screens to keep a small child in the house, Theda sometimes escaped into the neighborhood wearing her mother's hats and gowns. She was strong-minded so, when punished, she would become even more mischievous. She would use any means available to reach the door locks, and she even made a hole in the screen door so that she could escape.

The Goodmans erected a large cage-like enclosure in the backyard to prevent Theda from slipping away and wandering the streets. When she realized that she could not escape the enclosure she would fall into screaming fits. Throughout her life, and even after she became the world-famous Vamp, Theda still carried the resentment of being put, as she said, "in the cage." (Flashes of this resentment could sometimes flare, especially when she felt confined by her roles, or when she was upset with other actresses who were erroneously labeled "the original Vamp" by the press.) As little Teddy began to realize that "the cage" was unavoidable at this point in her life, she began to settle down and play quite happily in it.

Ida Dayberth, born in Ohio, was hired as a governess to teach Theda English and mathematics. Ida was a strong influence on Teddy's enjoyment of books and poetry. Anna Tusing, from Kentucky, was the Goodmans' housekeeper. Theda, at a young age, had the responsibility of translating her mother's household instructions into English for Ida and Anna. Theda admitted that she would give them instructions that her mother had not given! She would have Ida take her shopping to buy items that she wanted, and she also requested that Ida take her to the Tableau Vivant every week. The Tableau Vivant was a place where artists would strike poses and stand very still to create a living picture. It was considered a form of art to recreate a famous painting or a spectacular scene to exact detail. Many of the artists were scantily clad or posed in the nude. Needless to say, Ida was not easily fooled, and little Teddy did not always get her wish!

The Goodman children were provided a marionette stage and

many marionettes and puppets, which they used to perform backyard plays. Theda became jealous when the neighbors came to see one pretty little girl who could sing. At a gathering while this little girl was singing, Theda pushed the child out of the way and burst into song, while her mother cringed with embarrassment.

Another time a neighbor volunteered the use of his barn as a theater. Teddy immediately took advantage and created a one-person show. Cookies and lemonade were served as bribes to get the audience to pay "five pins" for entry. Theda performed a solo act made up of singing, dancing, and reciting, while her brother Marque served as pitchman, usher, and bouncer. He would position himself so as to trounce anyone attempting to leave. Although little Teddy loved to perform, she was shy. She feared rejection and she did not make friends easily. She was often excluded from children's parties.

In 1897, when Theda turned twelve, her Bat Mitzvah celebration was held at the Mound Street Temple. At the celebration she was to tell a story from the biblical Book of Esther about a Jewish queen from Persia. Theda arrived with her family properly dressed for the occasion. She slipped into a room and changed into a costume resembling one worn in Old Testament days. When it came time for her introduction, she appeared dressed in a thin wafting material which revealed her bare skin. To make matters worse, she was barefoot! The guests were quite shocked, as was Rabbi David Philipson. She was told to leave the room and change her clothes immediately, but little Theda stood her ground. She told the rabbi and guests that she could not and would not make her presentation without her period costume. (Theda later stated that even as a child she knew that the costume should reflect historical accuracy.) Then a serious little Teddy requested a reason for her interpretation's non-acceptance. It was reported that Mrs. Goodman slumped in her seat with embarrassment and nearly passed out. Carrying her second child, she went into labor and Theda's sister Esther was born there at the event. Theda's Bat Mitzvah was canceled. Later the congregation took a vote and agreed to allow Theda to wear her costume for the presentation. Her Bat Mitzvah celebration was rescheduled and took place in 1898. Teddy's presentation of the story of Esther, who would be queen, was so unusual that she was asked to present it again at the newly formed Women's Improvement Club of Cincinnati.

During her years at Walnut Hills High School, Theda was interested in psychology and mysticism. She was active in the drama club and appeared in the light comedies *The Lady from Philadelphia, American Beauties* and *An Exciting Day*. She also worked on the monthly newspaper, *The Gleam*. In her class photo, Theda is taller than most of her classmates because she was standing on a book. The entry next to her photo in the yearbook of 1903 states:

~Theodosia B. Goodman~
With heart and fancy all on fire,
To climb the hall of fame.

Theo excels in the literary art, and her work bears the stamp of a true genius. Her literary ability however is not the only claim she has to fame; her histrionic talent is characteristic and well known to those who have witnessed a performance of the senior dramatic club. She is an entertaining conversationalist.

After graduating from high school in 1903 at nearly eighteen years of age, Theda enrolled in the University of Cincinnati where she completed two years of study. It was at this time that her father suffered a serious injury to his hand and due to his inability to work, Theda stepped in. Under her father's supervision, she worked at Ochs, Weihl, and Goodman, Tailors, as an apprentice fabric cutter. When she was no longer needed, she assisted her mother at Dunkelmyer and de Coppet, Wig Makers.

At the wig shop, Theda became fascinated with the customers. Wigs at that time were worn as a symbol of social status and were customary for certain professions. Theda considered wigmaking to be monotonous because of the tying of thousands of strands of hair. But the craft paid very well and the shop attracted a wealthy clientele. She once said about the patrons, "A client with a balding head would come in and go out looking like a different person with a hair style that framed their face. An unattractive woman could be made beautiful with a change of hair color. Some clients had so many wigs they would be unrecognizable, a different person every day."

Theda realized that the customers wanted an illusion about themselves. She became obsessed with what was in a person's inner soul. Who were they really? Who did they want to be? How did they see themselves? While she was working tediously in the shop, she would daydream and imagine what the clients were like in a social atmosphere.

At home she brewed recipes for powders to cover blemishes, and color tones to match faces. She sold her own scented bath powder preparations in her mother's shop. She also made rose water to brew

1. Theda, the Early Years 11

Theda appears as the exotic Cleopatra in "a thin wafting material which revealed her bare skin." It must have reminded her of her appearance as a child in the role of a Jewish queen from Persia (Stout Collection).

a perfume. Theda started to apply makeup to the clientele, and in time she had more commitments than she could handle. She was so busy that the customers had to make appointments three or more months in advance.

Theda's own long flowing dark hair was used to her advantage in many of her films. From the film, *When Men Desire* (Stout Collection).

In February of 1906, Sarah Bernhardt, renowned stage actress of that era, boarded a ship to America for a farewell tour. She was provided a private rail car by the New York Vanderbilts in order to travel to the big cities. When she appeared at Cincinnati's Grand Opera House that year, Theda attended the performance. She was so inspired by Bernhardt's performance in Alexandre Dumas's play *La Dame aux Camillas* that she did not want to return to being a mere Cincinnati girl. She craved adventure and wanted to be on stage.

1. Theda, the Early Years

Omens of Luck

Under the name Theo Goodman, Theda enrolled into acting school in Chicago in the fall of 1906. This would be the first time that she would live away from home. When she arrived, she stayed in Milwaukee, Wisconsin, at the Schlitz Hotel. The Schlitz Hotel was famous for its Palm Garden, which was designed with mid–Victorian architecture and a domed interior. Inside were exotic plants, artificial ponds and fountains. The Garden was one of the most prestigious gathering places in the Midwest, attracting Hollywood celebrities and New York

Theda Bara, 1919. Photograph by Hoover Art Company, Los Angeles (Stout Collection).

Schlitz Palm Garden, Milwaukee, Wisconsin (Stout Collection).

socialites and their families. It had a seating capacity of 1000 people. The Schlitz Hotel was also adjacent to the most elegant tap room in the city.

One day Theda lingered outside the hotel's business office. The owner's son opened the door and asked her to come in. She later stated that she then offered him a suggestion: "Single ladies and gentlemen can't speak to one another unless they have been introduced. If you provide me a designated area I will guarantee that each person attending will be introduced by name to every attendee. I will put up a sign saying 'Singles Social Hour at 5:00 PM.' A small cover charge should cover my expense. I would like a free room at the hotel and a weekly salary." Theda later said to me that it was an "omen of luck."

The singles hour event became very popular with crowds of young people in line for the event each day. When Theda appeared, she had everyone form a single line. She led them into the room weaving snake-like in and out with her "jolly walk" that went like this:

> Put your hands on the waist of the person in front,
> Take three steps forward, kick with your right, wave with your right,
> Take three steps forward, kick with your left, wave with your left.
> (Repeat the last two lines.)
> Every other one, turn to your back, say your name and pass them around,
> Turn to the front, last and first step out of line, sit down, say your name.
> (Repeat.)

Around the tables they went until all had sat down and had been introduced. Theda said that she met many people and this was the most fun time in her life.

Milwaukee at that time was a vibrant city of live theater, nickelodeons, and beer parlors. The city attracted vaudeville, the best Broadway productions, and European touring companies. One of Milwaukee's top venues was the Pabst Theater. Built in 1895, it was ornately designed in the tradition of European opera houses, complete with a seating capacity of 1,345. Designed to be acoustically pure, it housed a 35 voice electro pneumatic pipe organ. Another theater, the Davidson, was popular because it attracted touring road shows. The Bijou Opera House, which opened in 1891, was the home for "mellow drama." However, the most popular theater in town was the exotic Schlitz Uihlein Alhambra Theater. With a seating capacity of 3,000, 18 luxurious boxes on three levels, and a large stage for vaudeville, it was the premier theater of the Midwest.

Theda thrived on living in luxury at the Schlitz Hotel. Because the

Theda Bara, April 12, 1916, the early years. Campbell Studios, New York (Stout Collection).

Davidson Theater was across the street, she attended every performance given by Sarah Bernhardt in the late fall of 1906. Bernhardt, a seasoned stage actress, could play any character presented to her, often playing both male and female roles equally well. Although she was noted for her repertory of classical French dramas, she was also known as "the woman who sleeps in a coffin and has pet snakes." She was identified as the most mysterious actress who crafted outrageous behavior and provocative stage performances.

By 1900, Bernhardt had achieved widespread fame in Europe and in 1906, Theda was most determined to make her acquaintance. She sent a note written in French requesting an interview with Bernhardt, stating that she was staying at the same hotel; therefore she could arrive at a moment's notice. She also stated in the note that there would be "no need for an interpreter." What Theda learned that day, she would never say other than that Bernhardt was the greatest influence upon her. One could certainly draw the conclusion that at this interview, Theda learned that sensationalism and publicity can insure good audiences.

While attending drama school and being hostess for the Schlitz singles hour, Theda also worked as a stage hand at the Pabst Theater. She was given a shareholder interest in the theater in exchange for monetary compensation. (I visited the Pabst Theater in Milwaukee after the death of Theda's last surviving family member, Lori Bara, to return the shareholder certificate that Theda had cherished throughout her life.)

Theda returned home for a Thanksgiving holiday visit in 1907. She had just walked into Dunkelmyer and de Coppet, Wig Makers, when Albert Mills came into the shop asking for a perfumer bath powder. Theda quickly put together a fragrant powder for him. He was so elated with the product that he stated he would send his carriage to take her to his office the following day.

Mills had launched the American Products Company in Cincinnati in 1907. It was a company that distributed household products door to door. He contracted with Theda, giving her ownership interest in the Zanol Lorens La Bara cosmetic line in exchange for Theda's perfumer powder recipe. This enabled her to receive a royalty payment throughout her lifetime. Theda said, "If I hadn't been at the shop at that moment, the opportunity would never have taken place." This was the day that her life changed so Theda considered this day an omen of luck.

2

Joan, the Early Years

California, Land of Dreams

My parents traveled west in 1939 from Erie, Pennsylvania, to establish the Craig Oil Company. It did not take much for my father to convince his family and friends to follow him; he had promised them that they would have a good time in California. They traveled by caravan from Erie across the continent with dreams of a future, and a desire to escape the Great Depression that had ravaged the nation. Because my grandfather did not trust banks, he brought suitcases full of silver certificates. After we arrived, my father was so busy finding locations and building gas stations that a permanent home for my family was not established.

By 1941, I was on the way to life and in June I was born. In October, I was handed over to a nanny, an American Indian nurse who smoked a corn pipe. I would often stay in her home on an Indian reservation outside of Reno, Nevada. The last time I saw her, she waved goodbye as she stood near her donkey and truck. When I had grown bigger, the backseat of the car became home while my parents drove from city to city. The El Rancho Hotel in Las Vegas became a familiar place. It was located on a corner when Las Vegas Boulevard was mostly just four corners.

My father ventured to put in a gas station next to the El Rancho Hotel. At that time the hotel was known for having an all-you-can-eat buffet. Food rationing did not apply there! The owner, Thomas Hull, owned a cattle ranch that supplied the hotel with beef and, most important for me, milk. Families with children were welcome. By 1946, I had traveled thousands of miles by car, thousands of miles by train, and I had even flown in an airplane. The hotels where we stayed were some of the finest of the day in California. I learned my way through the

Palace Hotel, the St. Francis Hotel, the Mark Hopkins Hotel, the Hotel Bel-Air, and the Beverly Hills Hotel, to name a few.

As I grew, I became accustomed to sitting in a high chair listening to singing entertainers and big band music. There were cowboys and Indians, western music and yodelers, and an easily imagined dance floor. However, the news broadcasts were not so carefree at that time. The news of a possible Japanese attack on San Francisco and the coastal areas increased. Travel became more difficult with shortages of gasoline, heating oil, food, and rubber. The West Coast had become a wartime theater of operations. Single lane highways were congested with caravans of military transports. Hotel rooms were hard to secure because they were reserved for the military and the roundup of enemy aliens on the West Coast.

We traveled everywhere with our English Sealyham Terrier. I remember being in a private sleeper rail car that was attached to the end of a troop train. Women were not allowed in the troop cars except for passing through and for dining. We were only seated in the dining car when it was empty.

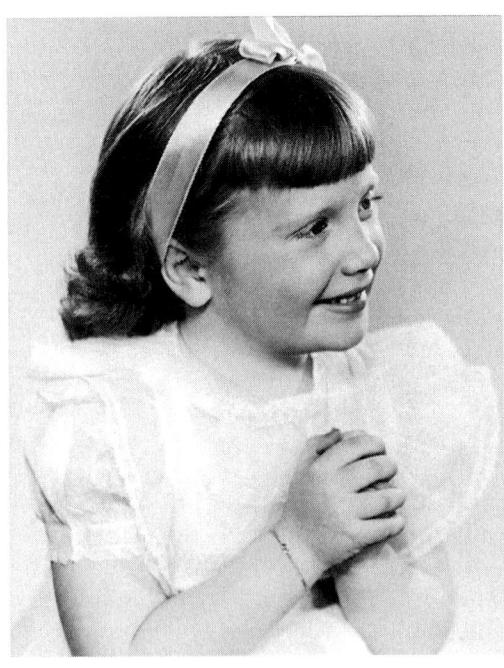

Joan Craig, 1945 (photograph provided by Joan Craig).

It was the beginning of 1946 when my parents finally decided to settle in Beverly Hills. A bridle path in the center of Sunset Boulevard extended past the Beverly Hills Hotel. People who lived in the canyon could ride their horses to the Beverly Hills Hotel or to town. A hitching post for horses was just past the main entrance to the hotel and the Beverly Hills Post Office had a hitching post at the end of the parking lot.

We moved into a rental house that was owned by the sugar king heir, Adolph Spreckels. My father had opened a Hollywood-style

John Craig and his father, James Reed Craig, founders of Craig Oil. They were the father and grandfather of Joan Craig (photograph provided by Joan Craig).

Craig Oil Company in the Miracle Mile section of Los Angeles. The station was the largest in the world in 1946, providing 24 pumps to its customers. During promotions, the Craigs would use large movie spotlights aimed at the sky to attract customers. It was a sight to behold (photograph provided by Joan Craig).

gas station in the Miracle Mile District, an affluent area under development on Wilshire Boulevard between Fairfax and Western Avenues. This was my father's dream, to build the largest gas station in the world. The station covered one whole city block and boasted having twenty-four gasoline pumps. The station was often ablaze with retired military search lights. Every other week at the Wilshire and Highland station was designated as entertainment night. This was when my dad gave away a brand new Cadillac to a lucky ticket holder. Needless to say, there were many cars lined up at our station to buy gas!

3

First Meeting

The Lady in the House

On my first day of school, I walked there with my nanny, Lillie. On the way, we passed a gentleman who was in his garden pruning his flowers. I said, "Hi, I'm going to school!" And with that remark, he said, "I have something for you." He cut a long-stemmed red rose and said, "Take this to your teacher." My hair was a golden red, I wore a red coat, and I had a red rose. From that day forward, my nickname was "Red."

Every day that I went to school I would cross the street to the house on the corner. The next time that I saw the gentleman, he introduced himself as Charles Brabin. He asked me to call him Uncle Charlie. Every time that I saw him, he would hand me a red rose for my teacher. One day Uncle Charlie told me that he was cutting the roses for the lady in the house. He said, "The lady in the house would like to meet you." It was then arranged for me to go to their house after school.

One afternoon I was taken to the entrance of their house. My nanny left me at the front door and told me that she would come back for me in one hour. The door opened and I was greeted by Uncle Charlie. He said, "Please come in." I walked into a circular foyer and he asked me to proceed into the living room. This was quite a large room full of very unusual furnishings, artwork and tapestries. Uncle Charlie knocked on a small door to the right and called out, "She's here." As I stood waiting, there was a sweet smell of incense and a black cat asleep on a chair.

A small woman appeared. She stepped forward towards me and stood for a moment. I went forward immediately to shake her hand and I curtsied. As I looked up at her she seemed to have a golden aura around her with the most haunting, penetrating brown eyes and a very sweet smile. There was something magical about her. She gestured

Charles and Theda Bara Brabin, c. 1922 (Stout Collection).

with her left hand and said, "Please sit here, and I will sit here on the couch." Uncle Charlie sat down next to her. The conversation started out almost like an interview. She said, "Now, please tell me your name." I said, "My name is Joan and my nickname is 'Red'!" She asked, "How

3. First Meeting

old are you, may I ask?" I said, "I'm five." "Are you going to school?" she asked. I said, "Yes."

Miss Blue, their housekeeper, appeared with tea, milk and cookies. Theda then said, "My name is Theda [pronounced Thayda]; however sometimes I am called Theda [pronounced Theeda]. My nickname is 'Moody'!" We all laughed. "But I call Charles 'Moody,' so it can be confusing." We laughed again.

Above the sofa where they both sat was a large portrait of Uncle Charlie sitting in a chair and looking very regal. On the table in front of Theda was a strange object that had a purple cloth over it. Every once in a while she would lift up the purple cloth and peek at it. I had been taught at home not to ask personal questions so I quivered with curiosity.

Theda said, "Now, dear, please tell me something about you." I wasn't sure how to answer since no one had ever asked me a question like that before. I told her that I lived up the street on the other end of the block. I rambled on and told her that someone had stolen my father's car. I said that I was in my parents' bedroom saying good night and when I looked out the window, I saw someone driving the car away. When I told my parents, they didn't quite believe me. I was very upset so I told them again that the car was gone!

Theda and Charles looked at each other. Uncle Charlie said, "She is like I told you." I continued talking. I told them that my

Charles Brabin (photograph provided by Joan Craig).

portrait was being painted and I had to sit very still and not move. Theda then asked, "Can you show me how you pose for the painting?" I told her that I had to sit on a high stool. Theda asked Uncle Charlie to bring in a stool. She said, "Now, show me." I climbed up onto the stool and showed her while explaining that I also held my doll. I said, "The artist, Eliasz Kanarek, keeps the painting covered and he won't let me see it until it's finished."

The next time I saw Uncle Charlie in his garden, I told him that my grandpa had died. He said that the lady of the house would like very much to see me. This time she was peering at me from the front door. "Come in," she said. Uncle Charlie told her my sad news. "Come over here. I

Portrait of Joan Craig by the Polish artist Eliasz Kanarek (photograph provided by Joan Craig).

want to show you something." With that, she pulled the purple cover off of her crystal ball. "Let's see if I can see your grandpa here. There are spirits and sometimes they appear there." She continued, "Do you know anything about fairies?" I shook my head. She said, "There are all kinds of spirits and sometimes they are called fairies. There are also guardian angels. Your grandpa may be one of them!"

I told Theda that I liked Peter Pan and that I wanted to fly like Peter Pan. Theda said, "Come, let's fly! Follow me!" She stepped forward

3. First Meeting 25

and raised her arms up and down and we danced around and around, flapping our arms and pretending we were in the sky. I now had a friend and a playmate. Beverly Hills was a lonely place. One would hardly see anyone walking, much less a child. Children were kept carefully guarded in their homes.

Upon leaving her home that day, Theda said, "I have something for you. Please put this under your pillow every night and when you lose a tooth, put it in this little pillow. I think that a fairy will visit you."

One morning soon after, I went into the family room of my home. The carpet was actually moving! I was very frightened. It was discovered that the room was full of termites! The whole house would have to be tented. We moved into a temporary house on Camden Drive in Beverly Hills, and this is when my front tooth finally came loose. I made such a fuss, having to have Theda's little pillow under my big pillow every night until finally, I was toothless!

Theda as a Fleurette, a ballet dancer in *La Belle Russe*, 1919. This scene is similar to Theda's Peter Pan dance with Joan (Stout Collection).

While living in the temporary house, my parents went away on a long trip. My grandmother had broken her ankle in a fall. My nanny, Lillie, had decided that she didn't like Beverly Hills. She thought that Beverly Hills was "spooky"!

I was left in the care of a nurse from an agency. One night I heard noises outside my door. I peered out of my room and saw men going into my parents' room. I was scared so I locked my bedroom door. The next morning I learned that we had been burglarized. The robbers had left a trail of my mother's clothes in the hallway. The police came and I told them that I saw two men. They asked me if my daddy was one of them! I told them that my father had a bald spot and the robbers had hair.

I did not walk past Theda's house any more since we had moved at least ten blocks away. I was devastated because I had lost my playmate. I was longing to tell Theda about the tooth fairy, and I didn't have a rose for the teacher. My grandmother took me to church on Sundays in hopes that I would find a friend. One day on my way into Sunday school, a lady asked me to take the hand of a little girl named Ava. We walked into Sunday school together, hand in hand. We became friends.

Soon after, my parents had a party. Amongst the guests were the Gabor sisters. Abalone, live crabs and lobsters were brought into the kitchen by Eva Gabor's husband, Charles Isaacs. The crabs got loose and were crawling around on the floor. Then Mr. Isaacs told me all about diving deep into the ocean in La Jolla. He later brought me goggles, a snorkel and fins.

My mother started looking at houses with a realtor. She liked a house that was a two-story and had a big swimming pool. The house was vacant with one exception: The realtor explained that the living room could not be seen because it was occupied by snakes! The owner did not want them caged.

The realtor showed us another house. This house belonged to Lucille Cavanaugh Leimert, the former stage and vaudeville actress and dancer, then a socialite and *Los Angeles Times* newspaper columnist. Mrs. Leimert had converted the dining room into a room with mirrors, ballet bars, and a wooden dance floor. She and her friend Theda Bara would practice all different types of dancing in this room to stay fit.

The house was filled with treasures from China. The realtor

explained that the tall gated doors off the garden were made of very old Chinese tiles that were valued at nearly as much as the price of the house. Mrs. Leimert's son, Walter Leimert Jr., had given his mother the beautiful treasures while acting as a radio correspondent with the CBS News team in the Pacific during World War II. My parents purchased the house that day.

Magical Move and Spirits

The moment came when I looked out the window of our new house and saw Uncle Charlie in his garden. I rushed outside and stood on the corner. Uncle Charlie came across the street and took me by the hand to go see Theda. Theda expressed her despair in not knowing why I had disappeared. She said, "The spirits and I have been working very hard for your return." I told Theda and Uncle Charlie that we had moved into the house across the street.

Theda said, "Come sit over here at the table by the window." She

Theda gazes into her crystal ball in *Salome*. She would continue to use it throughout her life (Stout Collection).

702 North Alpine Drive, the home of Mr. and Mrs. John Craig and Joan (photograph provided by Joan Craig).

lifted the purple cloth covering her crystal ball and said, "He is wagging his tail! The spirit in here is my dog and he never lets me down." As I gazed at Theda through the sunlight from the window, there was a golden hue of color surrounding her dark hair. I knew at that moment that she had a special power to bring me to her, but I dared not ask questions!

Theda told me all about her dear friend who had lived in the house across the street. She expressed how much she would miss her. Theda approached a pair of jade lamps with tall bases in her living room. The jade was exquisitely carved with little figures detailing early life in China. When the lamps were turned on, one could see all the various colors in the jade. Theda said she had acquired them from the lady when she moved. Uncle Charlie went over to light the lamps and said, "It probably took more than 100 years to create the story carved with the little figures in the jade stone." Theda described the tall gates in my garden, stating that they were made of ancient imperial jade.

At this time we were living in the house mostly without furnishings. A decorator came to our house every day and showed my mother all kinds of samples of materials and colors to decorate the house. She would tell the decorator that she had made up her mind on choices of fabric and paint. The decorator would arrive and the next day she would tell him that she had changed her mind. Finally I told my mother that I liked yellow and she seemed to go along with it. Yellow carpet was laid throughout the house.

4

Settling In

The Brown Derby

Theda and Uncle Charlie sent an invitation to my mother and grandmother for lunch at the Brown Derby in Beverly Hills. A special booth was reserved in the dining room for Theda and her guests. As we walked through the dining room, some people seemed to stare and whisper. Theda was walking serenely, and wearing a hat with her face covered by a veil. On the walls of the restaurant were black-inked, hand-drawn caricatures. One of them on the wall next to the kitchen I barely recognized as Theda. We were served the house special, a Cobb salad.

My grandmother spoke about the time when she took a train into New York City to see Theda in *The Blue Flame*—and that she dressed as a man in order to be admitted alone! This confirmed my thoughts that Theda was magical and that everyone must know. I started to ask about *The Blue Flame* but my mother nudged me to be quiet. My mother then explained to Theda and Uncle Charlie that she grew up in New Jersey not far from the Fox Studio in Fort Lee. She said to Theda, "I have always admired you." Theda smiled as if she was enjoying my family's accolades. Theda stated that this luncheon was for the benefit of "Red," and that she and Charles enjoyed my visits. During the lunch, people came shyly by, almost in fear to ask Theda to autograph their menu. I really didn't quite understand. While everyone was talking, I was staring. I could again see a golden color all around Theda. She was still very mysterious!

Flying Tigers

My parents and I went to a party at a stately home in Pasadena. It was a special party for Robert (Bob) Prescott. The house was full of

4. Settling In

The Brown Derby Restaurant, Vine Street and Hollywood Boulevard, 1950. Drawings of the stars can be seen on the walls (Bison Archives and HollywoodHistoricPhotos.com).

balloons and everyone was celebrating. It was announced that Bob Prescott had raised the large amount of $89,000 to start an air freight transport company. Sam Mosher, founder of Signal Oil and Gas Company, was there to hand him a check of matching funds to form the Flying Tiger Line, an airline freight company. I was told that I had witnessed a very important historical event!

My father made a simple request: He asked Bob to fly my grandmother's furnishings to California from New Jersey. This was just what Mr. Prescott needed, the proof that he could fly furniture. Everybody celebrated. I was sure that Theda had something to do with it.

The next day I told Theda and Uncle Charlie all about the party for Bob Prescott. I explained that our furniture would be arriving by an airplane. When Theda heard the name Bob Prescott she said, "Oh, I want to meet this great man! When the furniture arrives, let me know right away."

One morning the door bell rang and I opened the front door. There stood Bob Prescott, and in front of the house were several trucks. He said, "The furniture has arrived." Bob's face was ashen. He sat down on our front steps and wiped his brow. I told him, "Wait right here, someone magical wants to meet you!"

I ran across the street and told Theda that the furniture had arrived. She quickly came over and introduced herself. Bob said, "My plane took off in the fog and I nearly didn't make it. There were bad storms most of the way and it wasn't a very good landing either." What he meant was that the plane kind of fell apart on landing. Bob had made the historic flight in a Budd C-93 Conestoga, a war surplus plane carrying the furnishings. He said, "We need to thank the Lord that I got here!" By the tone in his voice I knew that he meant it. One has to imagine flying across the country at 165 miles per hour and running out of gas after 700 miles!

Late in the day my father took everyone, including the Brabins and Bob Prescott, to a Polynesian restaurant called The Tropics in Beverly Hills to celebrate. The next morning it was discovered that the Oriental tile gates at our house had been dismantled. The tiles were gone. We had been robbed again.

The Afterlife

On my next visit to Theda's, there were little sandwiches already on the table for me. I told Theda all about the loss of the jade tiled gates. She said, "Let's see why there is so much trouble." As Theda peeked under the purple cloth and looked into the crystal ball, she remarked, "Your father was born in Pennsylvania and your mother was born in New Jersey." She paused for a moment and said, "He is asking for more information. Do you know where or when they were married?" I said, "I think they are brother and sister." With that response she looked at me with a small smile. Theda then asked me if I knew anything about reincarnation. I told her that I didn't know the meaning of the word. She explained, "When you are born, a spirit from a past life is born with you. At the time of your birth your spirit chose your parents. It also means that your spirit parents are different from your birth parents."

I thought for a moment about what she was saying to me. I said,

"I believe I have seen my other parents!" Theda's eyes opened very big and she looked at me as if she was surprised by what I had just said. "Please tell me, dear, when did you see them?" I told her that I was at a picnic in a park that had swings and seesaws. I watched the children on the swings and when they were up in the air, I decided to cross the swing area. I started to run and I was hit by a child on the swing. I was knocked down and when I tried to get up, I was hit again. While I was knocked out, I saw a long tunnel and it seemed that I traveled through it. At the end of the tunnel, I saw a man and woman with their arms open to me. As I came closer I could see them. They told me that they missed me and loved me so much, they just had to see me again. They said that I must go back. I didn't want to go back. They said, "You must go back through the tunnel the way you came. You have not been there long enough! You will come to us after you have completed all of our instructions that we send with you."

Theda as Iza in *The Clemenceau Case*, 1915 (Stout Collection).

Theda listened to my every word and then looked at me with true understanding. She had not heard anything like this before. She seemed to glow with the same kind of warmth and love that I saw surrounding the people at the end of the tunnel. Theda and I now had a secret. We shared something about the afterlife!

Theda asked me if I had told anyone about this. I had: After the incident my mother took me to a church. I went into a room and they were talking about a father who was in Heaven. I told the preacher that I wanted to find the mother and the father. I immediately was taken away. When my mother arrived, there seemed to be a problem. I was asked, "Do you know this lady? What is her name?" I said, "That's Mommy."

Theda listened to me intently and then said, "I think you saw your guardian angels." She turned on some music to soothe me. We walked around the room swaying our arms, turning around, and having fun. I now had a friend who understood me. When I departed I was told that the back door was usually open during the day and that I was welcome to come over as I pleased.

I would slip over to their house almost every day, taking my favorite books with me. Uncle Charlie would read to me. Theda would sit there and observe; sometimes she would play the piano and sometimes we would listen to an opera.

When I would enter Theda's house it was like entering into a world of the past, and it was difficult for me to refrain from asking a multitude of questions. The large living room was relatively dark. There were various seating arrangements mixed with unusual furnishings; it was almost like being in a museum. A dark mahogany wood-paneled wall with a fireplace gave warmth and comfort to the room. There was a beautiful tapestry hung on the wall. Over a period of time I would learn about every object in the house.

The first room on the right was Theda's bedroom. When one entered her bedroom, they could see an antique dressing table with a long mirror, and lace doilies on the tabletops. There were many exquisite perfume bottles on display. Her queen size bed would usually have a very soft pink coverlet with baby pillows resting on larger pillows. A chaise lounge was in the left corner with a painting of the Madonna and Child on the wall. A doorway on the right entered into a small office with a window facing the garden.

The second room off the living room was Theda's music room. It had an upright piano, a wet bar, sofa and chairs, and on the floor there was a real tiger skin rug. Near the floor and cut into the wall was an arched door to a mouse house with a mouse and catnip for Puddy. When television became available, Theda placed a set in the room.

A large crafted dagger, with a card signed by the Mexican revolutionary, General Pancho Villa, hung at the end of the living room on the wall, near the arched entry to the dining room.

The dining room accommodated a buffet table and a dining table with seating for eight which could be expanded with a panel. There was a swinging door on the left that entered into a pantry with a sink and glass cabinets above. On the right side of the dining room there

4. Settling In

were double arched doors that opened onto a large enclosed lanai with walls and a high ceiling made of glass.

On the lanai were several statues of goddesses. These were interspersed with wicker furniture and a chair made with whale bone. Uncle Charlie's director chairs and an Egyptian mummy lay in the corner. There was a door on the side of the room that led to Uncle Charlie's bedroom. His room was comprised of a high boy dresser and a four poster bed. The room was filled with boxes, books, and file cabinets.

A human skeleton (photographed in "The Vamp," a 1914 publicity photo) hung near the kitchen door. Theda would move him around. Sometimes he would be sitting in the living room and other times in the lanai facing the window. He could even be in the bathroom!

Miss Blue lived in a room that was attached to the garage. She was an elderly woman with a British accent, true to her name, she was always blue and she rarely smiled. Miss Blue was always dressed in an English style conservative gray or white uniform.

Sometimes when I arrived, Uncle Charlie would be listening to the radio so I would sit and listen with him. One time he asked me if

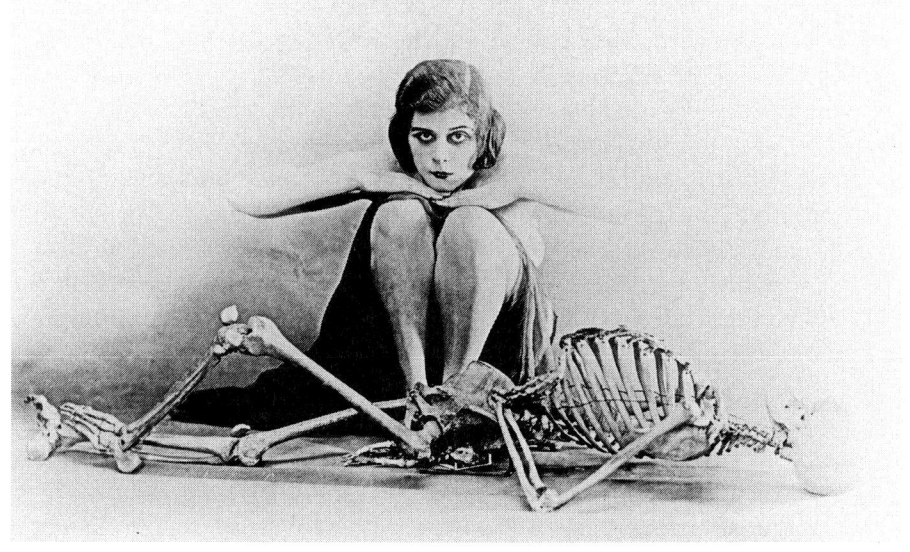

Theda in an iconic pose with the skeleton. The 1914 photograph sealed her onscreen (and sometimes off screen) persona as "The Vamp," a brand that made her career. Theda would lament it throughout her life (Stout Collection).

I had been to the movies. I replied, "No, I have never seen one." "Have you ever seen a cartoon?" he asked. I answered, "I have comic books." With that remark he brought out a book with lots of pages containing many drawings. He showed me that by fanning the pages the characters would move. He explained to me that this was how movies began.

Open House

My mother decided to have an open house party for all the neighbors. She gave me a handful of invitations to distribute. This friendly invitation might have been welcomed in a neighborhood in New Jersey but it certainly was not a custom in Beverly Hills.

The first house that I went to was the house behind us. A lady answered the door and she proceeded to announce to someone behind her, "A little girl is here with an invitation." A gentleman chewing on a pipe (Ben Hecht, an author and screenwriter known as the Shakespeare of Hollywood) came forward. He looked at the invitation and asked, "Are you Jewish?" I said I didn't know. Then he said, "You're not German, are you? What is your name?" He then led me over to a large table piled with papers and a typewriter. He said, "This is what I do. I write stories." He called out to Rose about the date. Then he said, "My wife will be away; I would appreciate a plate of food!"

I went to every house on our block on both sides of the street continuing to give out the invitations. I was looking for children but there were none. At the end of the street a lady opened the door who was pleased to have a visitor. She invited me in to see her house and then showed me an entrance into the ground that led to a bomb shelter. "When there are sirens," she explained, "you can come and stay in the bomb shelter with us!"

After leaving that house I went further than I had been allowed, to a house across the street from the school. This is where I had seen a tricycle. The family welcomed the invitation and said that they would bring their children.

The afternoon party was a great success. Payton, our cook, was from Baton Rouge, Louisiana. He made all kinds of Southern dishes including fried chicken.

My father John Craig, as a young boy, had played the piano for the silent films. When Theda arrived with Uncle Charlie, she was wearing

4. Settling In

Betty and John Craig, parents of Joan Craig. Joan's father delighted his guests with his music and sometimes played at parties given by the Craigs (photograph provided by Joan Craig).

a thin black veil over her face which she removed in our entry. My father was at the piano playing ragtime music. As Theda and Uncle Charlie entered our living room, my father switched to music relevant to Theda's films. His style consisted of part cabaret, part jazz, and dramatic ripples on the keyboard, all while keeping time with his left foot stomping the rhythm. Theda's face lit up with the biggest smile. She had not heard this kind of music for a long time.

John Tackaberry, along with his wife and children, were some of the first people to arrive. He was the writer of the funny lines delivered by Jack Benny on his radio show. Other neighbors who came were songwriters Harold Adamson and Sammy Fain, Cybil Brand, a philanthropist who lived alone with her white French poodle, and the popular children's dentist, Dr. Matthew Lasher. None of them seemed to know each other; however, friendships were made quickly.

A Croquet Garden Party

The Brabins soon had a garden croquet party honoring Robert Prescott and some of the American volunteer pilots who had provided air support for China against Japan during World War II. The Brabin house and garden were full of people. A mixture of celebrities, motion picture directors, and cinematographers stood anxiously waiting to converse with these brave men. The concept of a commercial freight air transport was naturally of great interest.

Some of the attendees included Ronald Reagan, Adolphe Menjou, Jeanne Crain, Fred MacMurray, Ava Gardner, Gene Lockhart, Maureen O'Hara, Bette Davis, Norma and Natalie Talmadge, and Henry Hathaway, the director of *Wing and a Prayer*. Charles Clarke also attended, bringing with him his daughter Mary. Clarke was the cinematographer for the 1946 Fox film *Margie* starring Jeanne Crain, and the Fox film *Miracle on 34th Street*, starring Maureen O'Hara, John Payne and Gene Lockhart.

Invitations to future gatherings were spread through casual conversations. Gene Lockhart would eventually entertain my family and the Brabins, with Bob Prescott being the honored guest. Norma Talmadge would also give a small dinner party honoring Prescott. At this time, Norma Talmadge was living in a house within walking distance of Theda's old home on Alpine Drive.

The Shadow of the Sphinx

The next time I appeared at Theda's, she asked me to sit at the table by the window in the living room. A statue of Budai, the jolly fat deity of

4. Settling In 39

Theda Bara reluctant to have her photograph snapped, c. 1940 (Stout Collection).

Chinese folklore, stood on the table. Theda pointed to the sack that he carried and remarked that he was smiling and laughing. She told me to rub his tummy and he would bring me wealth, happiness and prosperity.

Uncle Charlie was sitting close by in a chair when Theda asked, "Would you like to know where I was born?" I nodded. She stood and I followed as she walked towards the lanai. Dramatically she said, "I was born in the shadow of the Sphinx. I was the child of a princess. My father was an artist." She paused for a moment and held up her stuffed snake. "I was weaned on serpent's blood." Uncle Charlie, who was following us, could hardly keep from laughing. As we walked into the lanai, I could see that in the middle of the floor lay the mummy. All around the room was pictures of a sphinx, the desert, pyramids and camels. A globe sat on the table and a map was on the floor.

"Born in the shadow of the Sphinx": Theda in her most exotic role as Cleopatra, 1917 (Stout Collection).

4. Settling In 41

Theda with her stuffed snake in the film *The Serpent*, 1916 (Billy Rose Theater Division, The New York Library for the Performing Arts, Astor, Lenox and Tilden Foundations).

Theda pointed to a picture of a tent as she said, "I lived in a tent in the middle of the desert in Egypt." Then she pointed to the map of Egypt. I began to feel sorry for her. I could imagine how hot it must have been. She leaned against the door with her arm draped over her head and said, "I can't say any more!" She was upset. Uncle Charlie then referred to the map of Egypt on the floor, explaining that the globe was a map of the whole world. The mummy came from Egypt. Little by little, I was learning more about the mysterious woman who had both charmed and mortified audiences all over the world.

The sun was now setting earlier, and the light in the lanai was fading. There were strings stretched across the room with stars, the earth, the sun and the moon. The mummy had been moved to the side and replaced with Three Wise Men, a Buddha and an Aladdin's Lamp. A large star hung on the north wall, along with a picture of David with the Dove of Peace before it. Photographs of Roman ruins and other buildings had been added. Uncle Charlie showed me a compass and explained how it was used. I knew he must be a very smart man!

When I returned on another day, Theda pointed to the Star of David. She told me about the Mandala, or symbol of the hexagram, and how it represented the sacred union of "yin-yang." She also explained how the hexagram was comprised of two triangles which represented fire and water. Theda also taught me about the spiritual leader Buddha, and the significance of the Three Jewels, the three things that Buddhists look to for guidance. Over a period of time I learned about the symbols and the peoples of the world, the planets and their meanings, and the story of the magical Genie. I was told that the next time I visited, I must be able to recite the Ten Commandments. By doing so, I would learn about the prophet Moses and how he led his people through the desert in search of the Promised Land.

The next time I visited Theda and Uncle Charlie, it was the night before Christmas. Both of them were dressed in costumes. Dramatically they told me about Mary and Joseph and the Baby Jesus. They read to me the stories of Christmas!

Mansion on West Adams

A crème-colored Bentley with a red rose interior sat in the garage of the Brabins' home. Uncle Charlie said that the motor car

4. Settling In

Theda Bara in *The Soul of Buddha*, 1918 (Stout Collection).

(Uncle Charlie was from England) was a custom design made especially for Theda. I longed for a ride in it, but it never happened. I would see Uncle Charlie back the car into the street, then put it back in the garage. Once in a while he would drive Theda to a special occasion. This would require them to be in evening dress. Theda would wear a corsage on her wrist and Uncle Charlie would wear a flower in his lapel.

One day Uncle Charlie and Theda hired a car and driver. I was invited to go with them to see Theda's former residence. It was a stately Tudor style mansion located at 649 West Adams Boulevard in downtown Los Angeles. At the time, I was told that the neighborhood consisted of socially prominent people such as oil barons, developers and bankers.

Theda paused for a long moment as she stood in the room. She

649 West Adams Boulevard, the home of Theda Bara (Stout Collection).

said, "I had a large grand piano over there," as she was remembering her furnishings. Theda remarked that she did not live alone; her mother, father and sister also were there. I now understood and believed that after Theda grew up in a tent in the desert, she moved here!

We climbed the stairs and went into the bedrooms. She stood for awhile in the master bedroom and looked out the window with the view of the garden. She remarked that little had changed and the wallpaper was still the same. We went to the garden. Theda walked near the side of the neighbors. "Here is where I found my beautiful dog dead," she lamented. Some tears rolled down Theda's face and at that moment there was silence.

While viewing the interior of this extraordinarily large home, Theda remarked that neighbors were afraid to visit her; she had sent invitations to all of them. On one occasion the garden was filled with tables, decorated with white table cloths and flowers. There was food for a hundred guests. "Only a handful of people came," she stated. "I realized I could not live here any longer."

Theda's home was later occupied by Roscoe "Fatty" Arbuckle, director Raoul Walsh and his wife Miriam Cooper, and studio mogul Joe Schenck and his wife Norma Talmadge.

4. Settling In

Edendale and Cleopatra

The Brabins' driver drove us to see the location of the old Edendale Studios which is now in the neighborhood known as Echo Park. The area at that time was very beautiful with orange groves and views of the snow-capped mountains. It is where, in 1917, the film *Cleopatra* was made starring Theda Bara. This was a sad day for Theda; she was deep in thought about her life. As we drove, her eyes were glued to the views of Echo Park Lake. It seemed that she had not returned to this area for a very long time. As we proceeded from the car and into the park area, Theda described to us the filming of *Cleopatra*. She walked to areas in the park where many photos of her had been taken. She also walked to the location where she remembered standing in her Cleopatra costumes during the filming.

When we returned from the trip to Edendale, I was invited into Theda's house to view the movie *Cleopatra*. Theda and Uncle Charlie kept many films in a storage area in the basement of their house. This was to be a big moment, and Theda was very excited. She wanted this movie to be the very first movie that I would see. Uncle Charlie carefully removed the reel from its canister, placed it in the projector, and flipped the switch. Very quickly there was a puff of smoke! On the screen was a blotch that kept getting bigger and bigger. The projector kept turning and Uncle Charlie immediately turned off the switch.

Theda and Uncle Charlie were very upset. Theda screamed out in despair, "This is karma! There is noth-

Theda as the Queen of the Nile from the film *Cleopatra*, 1917 (Stout Collection).

ing left of my work!" She went to her room and would not come out for days. Uncle Charlie was very sad and concerned. He brought up other reels from the basement. One by one he opened them and he said that they all were unusable. Uncle Charlie began accumulating a list of possible theaters and other locations that may have copies of the films. I would post letter after letter and take them to the postal box on the corner. The replies to the letters always came back negative. Theda would lament the loss of her films for the rest of her life.

Theda Shops at Home

Theda would not allow Uncle Charlie to have any money in his pocket. He would have to get her permission for money expenditures. She would purchase fruits and vegetables from a truck that would come through the neighborhood twice a week. A delivery from Manning's Beef was made once a week.

I perceived that the Brabins were unable to purchase canned goods, so one day I decided to take all the cans out of our kitchen and sell them on the street corner. I invited Theda and Uncle Charlie to come shop. This event delighted Theda!

Theda as Cleopatra, from the 1917 film (Stout Collection).

The Brabins, Mae, and Sid

Shortly after the canned goods sale I was invited to have lunch with Theda and her dear friend Mae Murray, also known as "the girl with the bee-stung lips." Mae had

4. Settling In

begun her career as a dancer. She partnered with Rudolph Valentino back when his name was Signor Rodolfo. Rudolph Valentino was cast in his first lead part at the request of Mae Murray in the 1919 film *The Delicious Little Devil*.

Mae would make Theda laugh and there seemed to be great rapport between the two. During lunch one day, Mae told Theda to stop the despair over her lost films and start writing a book about her life. Theda's face brightened with the idea. Mae also suggested that Theda take me to see Grauman's Chinese Theater.

Theda was excited about writing a story about her life and she began to pull out photos from boxes that had been stored in the cellar. Theda and Uncle Charlie realized that it was very difficult to explain to me what a movie was since I had never seen one. They would lay out pictures for me to look at, then explain about the various people and places in the pictures. Theda and Uncle Charlie also impressed upon me the importance of details in the photos because certain details could be applied to a set design or a costume.

The next day, Theda and Uncle Charlie arranged for a limousine and driver to take me to see Grauman's Egyptian Theater in Hollywood. The theater had a long outdoor entrance. Upon arrival, I was told to walk with importance and to walk in the middle of the path. As we proceeded, Theda and Uncle Charlie reminisced about the grand opening of the theater. Uncle Charlie went to the spot where Theda had stood on that day. When we arrived at the theater entrance with its massive columns, we were met by Sid Grauman. Mr. Grauman warmly greeted Theda and Uncle Charlie and then took us on a tour of the theater.

After the tour, Mr. Grauman joined us in the limousine to go to his Grauman's Chinese Theater. Mae Murray was waiting for us at the theater. Mr. Grauman took us on a complete tour including the balcony and projection booth. He liked to talk about the costs of building the theaters and he enjoyed reminiscing about their openings. There was a hint of sadness as the three relived some past moments. The conversation became especially animated as they reminisced about the unexpected riots at the grand opening of Grauman's Chinese Theater on May 18, 1927. It was hailed as "the most spectacular theater opening in motion picture history"; it's estimated that thousands of people showed up and riots broke out as patrons fought to get a glimpse of their favorite movie stars and celebrities. As we entered the theater,

Uncle Charlie walked to the first landing on the staircase to the balcony. He said, "We were here when we began to be crushed by the hysterical crowd."

The interior of the theater was a magnificent recreation of a Chinese palace. Later the Depression caused great financial losses to the theater business that would never be recovered. Mr. Grauman sold his interest in the theaters. He remained as managing director until his death. He remarked that he was grateful for each day that he was there; "As you know, things can change overnight." Theda then asked Mr. Grauman for any information that he may have to locate the whereabouts of any of her films that may have survived.

As we departed from the theater, we walked past the handprints and footprints imprinted in some of the squares at the entrance. We stopped to view Theda's dear friend Norma Talmadge's footprints. Mr. Grauman remarked that the prints had happened by accident and that he had just left them there. It upset Theda to see her friend's footprints there and not her own. As we departed, Theda remarked, "The reason my handprints and footprints aren't there has to do with karma!" Again Theda's reference to karma would surface, as it did often during our conversations.

After the tour of the theater, we proceeded to C.C. Brown's Ice Cream Parlor, an old-fashioned parlor with high-backed booths and black walnut and mahogany tables. C.C. Brown was the inventor of the hot fudge sundae. As we were enjoying the sundaes, a few people came to the table and asked Theda for autographs.

Mae and Theda would often encourage each other to write their memoirs. Mae said to Theda, "Now you have a child to tell your story. This is what has been missing in your life! I long for my son but there isn't anything that I can do about it. There isn't a day that goes by that I don't think about him." I heard Theda say, "She brightens our day when she visits." I was beginning to understand that their lives had very exciting moments but there was a down side to being a star. As we departed, Mae said, "We can always meet at the Masquers Club just around the corner from Grauman's!"

Invite a Friend

It was arranged for Theda and Uncle Charlie to take me to a movie theater in Santa Monica to see *The Yearling* starring Gregory Peck and

Jane Wyman. They asked me if I would like to invite a friend. I said I would like to invite Ava Astaire. Uncle Charlie said, "Oh, her father is a dancer!" I said, "No, we think he is a gardener!" Uncle Charlie had such a surprised look on his face! He must have realized that I probably believed that he was a gardener as well!

Theda as Lolette in *The She-Devil*, 1918 (Stout Collection).

Audition

I entered first grade in the fall of 1947. Theda encouraged me to make up a little play. I created a play about my shadow. Uncle Charlie said, "Some time soon, someone will come to your classroom to take you to the school's stage. You can perform your play. And this is our secret and you should not discuss this with anyone including your family." The moment came. A teacher came to the door of my classroom and escorted me through the halls to the stage. I was told to walk to the front middle of the stage. The lights were very bright and I could not see anything beyond the edge of the stage. I was asked several questions, one of them being, "Why are you here?" I responded that I was there to tell them about my shadow! I managed to cover most of the stage as I performed, and I finished with a curtsy. The crowd of people stood up and applauded. The lights came on and I could see Theda and Uncle Charlie in the audience. Then I was escorted back to my classroom.

Unknown to me, this was an audition. Several months later when I came home from school, my mother said, "Your father had a phone call today. You've been offered a contract with MGM Studios to be in a movie. The caller declined to declare how you were chosen and they did not disclose any other information. Your father and I are upset about this and we have turned it down."

I wasn't disappointed, but I knew Theda and Uncle Charlie would be very upset. I really didn't have an interest in becoming a star and I didn't quite understand what all the fuss was about. I was more interested in observing the adults, listening to their conversations, and finding out what they were going to do next. I was quick to learn the names of people that I met, and I had learned to observe something about the person so that I could remember a face with a name. Theda had taught me to do that.

5

Remembering

Fortune

Theda was sitting at a table reading her fortune in the newspaper when she said, "I will show you how you can read your fortune. First you must write out your real name. Then look here; there is a number by each letter. When you add all the numbers in your name, that number will give you your fortune."

I printed out my name and placed the number on top. Theda said, "Now add the first two numbers together and put the numbers on the page." I quickly added the numbers on my fingers and wrote the number. "Now continue, and write the numbers in a column until you have used all the letters in your name. You must make sure that the numbers are correct to read your fortune."

Quickly I added the numbers on my fingers, then put the numbers in a column and added them again. Theda pointed to the number in the newspaper and said, "Read your fortune and by doing this every day you will gain a fortune!" I did this every day and I was placed in second grade. I had gained a fortune.

Gable, Fleming and Bergman

My mother and Theda loved to give parties. Theda gave instructions to Miss Blue to make various appetizers which always included stuffed celery, deviled eggs, caviar with crackers, and ham spread with sweet pickle. Our cooks Payton and Ann, being from near New Orleans, always prepared a superb buffet of Southern foods.

A party at the Brabins was given in honor of Ingrid Bergman. The play *Joan of Lorraine* was a big success on Broadway and the Joan of Arc story was a sought-after property for a movie. Bergman had flown to Los Angeles for an overnight stay with an immediate return to New York City the following day.

Some of the guests who arrived were Lee Garmes, cinematographer of *Gone with the Wind*, and his wife, actress Ruth Hall. Also in attendance were Clark Gable, Victor Fleming, Walter Wanger and his wife, Joan Bennett, Buddy De Sylva, Rosalind Russell and her husband, Danish-American producer, Frederick Brisson, Kay Williams Spreckels, wife of sugar heir Adolph Spreckels II, Count Sophus Danneskjold and his wife, actress Nina Romano, and astrologer Carroll Righter. All had come to honor Ingrid Bergman.

Clark Gable and Victor Fleming showed up together after most of the other guests had arrived. Ingrid was sitting on the sofa with Theda. When Gable and Fleming entered the house, they brought life to the party. They soon retreated to the back of the room with their drinks. Mr. Fleming made a remark to me about the beautiful color of my reddish blond hair. He said, "I bet that color can't come out of a bottle!" I said, "My name is 'Red'!" He then said, "I'm starved, where's the food?" I liked Mr. Fleming instantly. When he spoke, he looked directly into your eyes.

I led them into the dining room. Payton and Ann were removing the plates from the table. I told Payton that they were hungry. I continued to stand near Mr. Gable and Mr. Fleming, listening to their conversation while they were waiting. The men seemed to have a great friendship and they joked a lot with each other. Then I heard Mr. Fleming tell Mr. Gable that he was enamored with Ingrid Bergman. Mr. Gable then said, "What about the one with the powder blue eyes that just came in?" Mr. Fleming remarked, "Those eyes are to die for!" (They were referring to Kay Spreckels.) Mrs. Spreckels had been invited to the party by my parents. She was my father's neighbor when they lived in Pennsylvania.

Payton brought full plates of food to Mr. Gable and Mr. Fleming, which they devoured as if they had never seen food. They continued joking while they were eyeing everyone in the room. Mr. Fleming focused his eyes on Ingrid Bergman and said, "I'm in love with her, Clark. Are you interested in Ingrid? If you are, I'll step back." Mr. Gable said, "No, I'm not ready for that. I'm still a bit down." While

5. Remembering 53

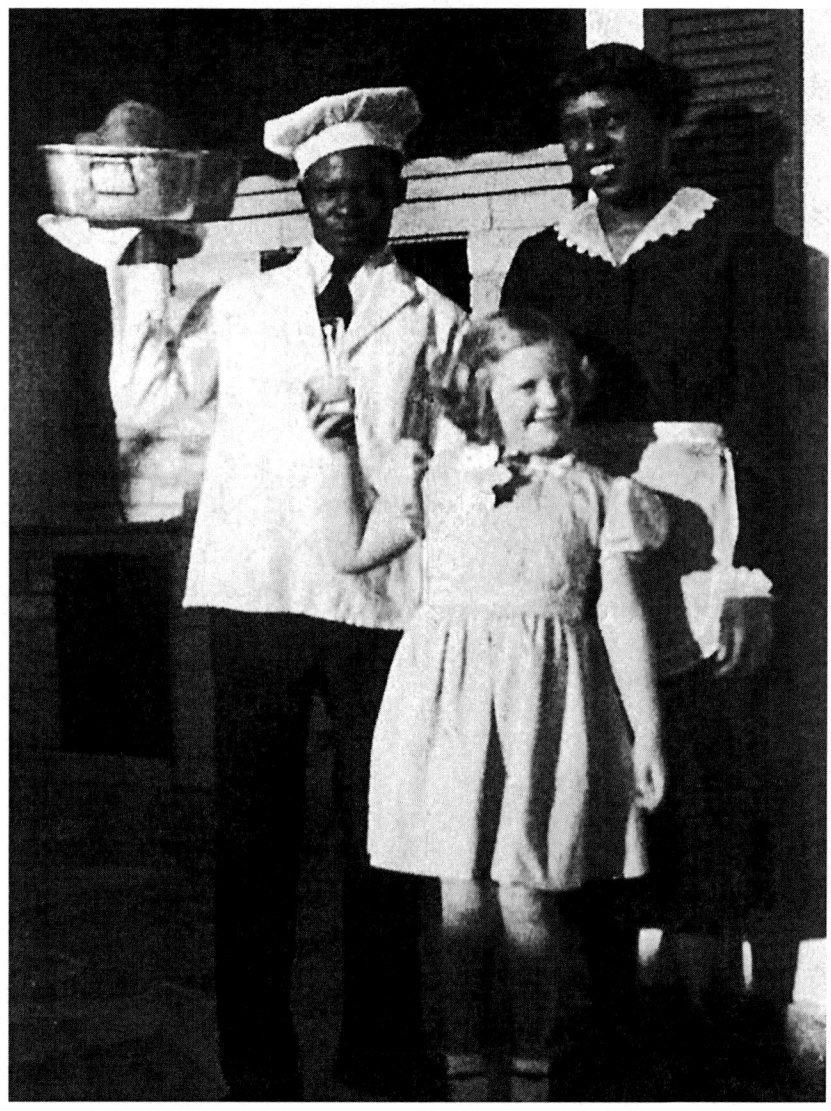

Joan with cooks Payton and Ann, c. 1947. A turkey had been prepared for the guests (photograph provided by Joan Craig).

Mr. Fleming stood there he seemed to quiver with excitement. He remarked, "I shouldn't be doing this. Okay, Clark, I shouldn't, but I'm going for it! Are you ready? Let's go join them. You take blue-eyes!"

The words, coming from a man saying that he was in love, made a big impression on me. With his expression and tone of voice I could feel his emotion. I already knew a little about love. I had seen Uncle Charlie with love in his eyes crown Theda Bara as Cleopatra. That memory couldn't have been more loving and true.

As Mr. Gable and Mr. Fleming proceeded back into the room to mingle with the guests, I watched them closely. I had just heard Mr. Fleming exclaim that he was instantly in love. It was like a drama unfolding.

Mr. Gable joined the conversation with Rosalind Russell and her husband. Mr. Fleming went graciously and directly towards Theda Bara, as she was conversing with Ingrid. Mr. Gable continued to mingle until he was introduced to Kay Spreckels, who would years later become Mrs. Clark Gable.

Carroll Righter, originally an attorney from Salem, New Jersey, had become well known as the astrologer for Hollywood celebrities. He liked to introduce people by their signs. Every month he would have a party, inviting guests according to their astrological sign. He would often have a real lion as a guest for his Leo parties. Theda was delighted to have Mr. Righter at her party. He would soon be consulted by the Brabins regarding the best date and time for the significant parties to sign movie contracts.

The gathering was a great success. Everyone was very excited about the possibilities of filming *Joan of Arc*. As the guests began to leave, I noticed that Mr. Gable departed with Kay Spreckels. Ingrid Bergman said that she had to board a flight back to New York. As Mr. Fleming departed, he stated that he was going to New York to see Ingrid's performance in *Joan of Lorraine*, and would return in a few days. Mr. Fleming turned to Uncle Charlie and said, "I will meet with you here and this shall be our meeting place." Mr. Wanger agreed that it would be best to meet at the Brabins.

Mr. Fleming returned in a few days, and a meeting with Uncle Charlie, Theda, Walter Wanger and Lee Garmes took place. I, of course, was somewhat included since I was there. Mr. Fleming stated that Ingrid would commit to making the film. He said, "There is not a lot of time to pull this together and if we can't get it together, Ingrid will accept some other offer. She wants ownership and will put up some money. I have already lost track of what day this is. Are we in the month of February or is this still January? When is Easter? Ingrid told me that

5. Remembering

she was invited to an awards dinner and I have an idea that she will be presented with an award." Wanger then said, "The closing of Maxwell Anderson's *Joan of Lorraine* on Broadway will be May 10." (This conversation took place in 1947.)

Before they arrived, I had helped Uncle Charlie gather from his files, pictures of scenes of medieval life that would be appropriate for the movie. Mr. Fleming glanced at the scenes and said, "I want more of this but I have to get an idea of the costs." Mr. Wanger turned to Lee Garmes and asked, "Are you in?" Mr. Garmes declared that he was already committed to an Alfred Hitchcock movie. He stated that he would help all that he could. They continued discussions regarding the movie being filmed in Technicolor.

Everyone walked across the street to our house for dinner. While dining, they discussed the idea of having Maxwell Anderson write the screenplay. There were concerns regarding the length of time that it would take to adapt the play for the big screen.

Also in attendance at the dinner were my mother's in-laws from her first marriage, Kay Harrison and his wife Heather. They were staying in a cottage at the Beverly Hills Hotel. It was just by luck that Mr. Harrison was in Beverly Hills at this time. He was the managing director of Technicolor Films in London, Paris, and Rome. Filming techniques were changing rapidly, and the development of Technicolor was a major advance for the industry. Mr. Harrison served as a liaison for communications between the film industry's needs

Theda Bara, elegant and beautiful, c. 1920 (Stout Collection).

and Technicolor. He was the go-to person when difficulties arose over filming in Technicolor.

Bergman as Joan of Arc

On February 1, 1947, the *Los Angeles Times* reported the following: "Direct from New York Wire, Edwin Schallert publishes the Ingrid Bergman announcement that she will play the role of Joan of Arc in a Technicolor picture, which she will make independently in association with Victor Fleming, the director, and Walter Wanger, the producer. The film will go into work as soon as Maxwell Anderson's *Joan of Lorraine* closes."

Sierra Pictures was formed with Walter Wanger, Victor Fleming and Ingrid Bergman listed as corporate directors. This would be the only film produced by Sierra Pictures. There were still concerns regarding the costs and Wanger wanted to raise additional funds for reserve.

All of the excitement and activity regarding the filming of the movie brought smiles to Theda and Uncle Charlie. Uncle Charlie seemed to forget that he was recuperating from a surgery. I helped Uncle Charlie with his files of clippings, which were of various scenes and costume prints. Theda was also very busy gathering period photos. She showed me a costume that was very heavy with armor.

Theda brought out of her room a very old book titled *The Personal Recollections of Joan of Arc* by Mark Twain. Theda and I read this together. I now wanted to use my real name Joan instead of 'Red'! I learned to read well with this book and I read the story over and over. Joan of Arc was indeed the deliverer of France!

In March of that year, Fleming and Wanger appeared at the Brabin home for a meeting. Although Wanger was gracious and mild-mannered, he was not pleased with the script. There were discussions about Andrew Solt being the person to help Anderson adapt the story to the screenplay format. Uncle Charlie told Wanger that Solt would accept the offer. The other concerns were with filming locations due to a tight budget. Wanger and Fleming glanced at the suit of armor that Theda had placed on a chair and then looked at the array of photographs and clippings that Theda had placed on the table. Upon picking up the costume, they found it to be very heavy. At that moment Mr. Fleming realized that the weight of the costume would be a problem. He remarked, "Ingrid would never wear anything like that." He then directed Uncle Charlie to make a note to call Western Costume Company, saying, "They should have a lot of period costumes. We better reserve them now! I'm leaving for New York in a few days!"

A Masquerade Party

On March 15, 1947, Theda wore her peacock dress that she had designed for the film *Cleopatra*. Just days before the party, she had brought out her castanets and dress, and we danced around the room. Then she told me to sit in her queen's chair as she explained the history of Queen Esther, Haman, and the Celebration of Purim. I was again given instructions on how to remember a face with a name. Theda said, "On the day after the party, I want you to tell me the names of the guests and how you identified them."

Theda, Uncle Charlie and I greeted the guests as they arrived in costume. When Theda moved about to mingle, I carried her long peacock feathered train.

Theda was magnificent in her costume, with a form-fitting dress and a trail of blue green peacock feathers. To me, the guests became almost ordinary in their costumes! Theda then asked everyone to join her in the Celebration of Purim. Most of the guests were not familiar with the Jewish celebration, so I passed a card to each group of three guests giving instructions as to when to shout "boo," "cheer," "hiss," stomp feet and ring the noisemakers in unison. Theda, on cue, ceremoniously unfolded a scroll from Queen Esther to recount the story of Esther. However, when she started to read from the scroll everyone became confused. It seemed like none of the guests in the groups could follow the instructions. When someone cheered or booed at the wrong time, Theda would have to start over reading from the scroll. However, each time a mistake was made, everyone laughed.

The party was a feast. The dining room table was set with all the food that Theda had made, with one exception: the stuffed grape leaves which came from a special place on Hollywood Boulevard. Items on the menu included cinnamon wine soup, brisket of beef, poached fish, liver pate, folded triangle dumplings in soup, and braided bread. There were also little folded cookies with apple, prune, and strawberry, and

Theda in the famous peacock dress from *Cleopatra*, 1917 (Stout Collection).

honey nougats with walnuts and baklava. On the side table stood two gifts for one friend.

The guests that came were a true cornucopia of Hollywood elites: Raoul Walsh, Herbert Brenon, King Vidor, Francis X. Bushman, Robert Cummings, Spencer Tracy, Edward G. Robinson, Thurston Hall, Boris Karloff, Maureen O'Sullivan, Angela Lansbury, Elsa Lanchester, Charles Laughton, Marion Davies, Mae Murray, and Larry Parks, who came as a clown. (Thank goodness Theda taught me to remember the names of all the guests!) At the close of the party, Theda had the guests form a single line and then led them to the front door stepping to the kick of the Rumba.

Easter in Beverly Hills Hotel

On April 6, 1947, the Beverly Hills Hotel was the place to be for Easter brunch. Limousines were not used to make an entrance because the main access was blocked and under construction. The diverted route was through a garage, up an elevator, and down a corridor of rooms to the dining room. In spite of all this, celebrities along with their children managed to get there for the Easter Egg Hunt.

Seated at our table were the Garmeses and their daughters Pamela and Carol, Theda and Uncle Charlie, and the Harrisons. Victor Fleming, while passing our table to join his family, stopped to whisper that Ingrid Bergman was being presented with a Tony Award for her performance in *Joan of Lorraine* at a dinner in the Grand Ballroom of the Waldorf Astoria Hotel that same day. This was the first time in history that Tony Awards were presented. Although Bergman went on to be nominated for an Oscar for *Joan of Arc*, she lost to Jane Wyman for her work that year in *Johnny Belinda*. *Joan of Arc* did win two Oscars, one for Best Color Cinematography and one for Best Color Costume Design.

Communism in Hollywood

On April 10, 1947, Ronald Reagan (then the Screen Actors Guild president) and his wife Jane Wyman, provided the names of Screen Actors Guild members who were believed to be Communist sympathizers according to the FBI.

The Biltmore Hotel in downtown Los Angeles became the stage for interviewing friendly witnesses and celebrities. At this meeting, the Motion Picture Association of America interviewed fourteen friendly witnesses who were willing to testify about Communism in Hollywood. Some of those witnesses were Robert Taylor, who had starred in *Song of Russia*, and co-writers Paul Jarrico and Richard Collins. Some members were angry about scripts with words such as "tender comrades," "share and share alike," and "that's democracy."

Adolphe Menjou had formed a group called the Motion Picture Alliance for the Preservation of American Ideals. On May 9, 1947, the second day of the "friendly" interrogations, Theda Bara, Uncle Charlie and I entered the Biltmore Hotel as guests of Menjou. The main entrance lobby was full of people. Cameras were everywhere. People were at microphones giving interviews. We were escorted up the stairs to the convention rooms. As we entered the hallway outside the rooms, we could see where people were gathered. Menjou was there to greet

Theda, left, and singer Yaeckel Louis attend a Hollywood dinner at the Writer's Club in honor of Walt Disney, creator of Mickey Mouse and the Silly Symphonies, September 29, 1933 (© 1935 The Associated Press).

us. There were a lot of people going in and out of doors and photographers were everywhere.

Juanita Freston and her husband Herbert Freston, counsel for Warner Brothers, also came forward to greet us. I took Theda's hand and stood next to her. Many people were surprised to see Theda there. Just before the lunch break, Menjou escorted the Brabins and me into the Biltmore Bar and Grill Restaurant.

When we returned from lunch, the atmosphere in the hallway had changed. People were quietly talking about what they had heard in the closed-door room. It was nearly time for the announcement by Jack L. Warner listing the names of unfriendly witnesses, also known as the Hollywood Blacklist. While we were waiting, Theda posed as if she were talking to someone in order to carefully observe the crowd. Uncle Charlie stood in a way that he could see everyone. We were then ushered into the room and were present for Warner's announcement.

On May 19, 1947, car after car left the driveways of Beverly Hills homes heading towards the Gilmore Stadium. It was a foggy evening.

I, along with my parents and the Brabins, were there to attend a mass rally. Former Vice-President Henry Wallace announced that he was amazed at the extent of "Red infiltration" in the movie studios. Katharine Hepburn (in a red dress) made a surprise appearance to warn the people with her articulate voice and powerful words:

> I want to speak to you about the attacks on culture. I speak because I am an American and as an American I shall always resist any attempt at the abridgement of freedom. Silence the artist, and you silence the most articulate voice the people have. Destroy culture and you destroy one of the strongest sources of inspiration from which a people can draw strength to fight for a better life.

Katharine Hepburn's speech was very powerful and I listened to every word. She had sent a very important message that foggy night. Each and every word was spoken articulately. Ms. Hepburn had made her position crystal clear.

A Night to Remember

My cousin, Nina Romano, and her husband Count Sophus Danneskjold hosted a dinner party at their ranch in the San Fernando Valley. Their home was a secluded Tudor stone mansion with an adjacent breeding ranch for horses, consisting of approximately sixty acres. The grounds were soon to be subdivided into parcels for tract homes.

Nina's first marriage was a scandal. Sarah Bernhardt's matinee idol, Lou Tellegen, fell in love with Nina in 1923 while they were appearing in the melodrama *Maria Rosa*. At that time, Tellegen was married to the famed opera singer Geraldine Farrar. He married Nina the day after his divorce from her was final.

Lou and Nina had a child named Rex, whose birth had been kept a secret for fear that the news of his birth would damage his parents' careers. After four years of marriage, Tellegen and Romano divorced and she married Danneskjold. Rex was kept away from Hollywood influences on the ranch of his mother and stepfather. By the age of 22, Rex resembled his handsome father, and was just learning about his parents' theatrical past.

On an early afternoon in June 1947, Victor Fleming and Ingrid Bergman arrived at the Danneskjold ranch. They toured the property with Rex, in hopes that it would serve as a good location for the *Joan of Arc* set.

Bergman could see that the property and the Tudor stone mansion, complete with carriage house, would be an appropriate setting. Bergman and Fleming then enjoyed a long stroll, accompanied by Rex. They enjoyed seeing the horses and fowls grazing in the paddocks. Rex was a romanticist and found that being in their company was exhilarating.

A buffet table and several circular tables were set up on the veranda for the guests to dine. The veranda was enchanting on a balmy evening with the sparse twinkling lights of the valley in the distance and the Santa Monica Mountains as a backdrop.

Among the other guests to arrive that afternoon were Charles Brabin and Theda Bara, Bergman's husband Peter Lindstrom, Freddie Brisson and his wife Rosalind Russell, Clark Gable, Walter Wanger and his wife Joan Bennett, Constance Bennett and her husband General John Coulter, Jose Ferrer, Maxwell Anderson, and Carroll Righter.

When Bergman and Fleming returned from their walk to join the other guests, my eyes were on Mr. Fleming. He was magnetic and enthusiastic, and he spoke with authority. Carroll Righter stood greeting the guests by their astrological sign. Theda, still very beautiful and mysterious, engaged in conversation, encouraging others to talk about themselves.

Ferrer was in attendance that afternoon because he had been chosen to play the lead role of the Dauphin in the movie. He was selected because of his sensational appearance on Broadway as Cyrano in *Cyrano de Bergerac*. The American Theater Wing presented their first Tony Awards in 1947 for excellence in theater. Jose Ferrer and Ingrid Bergman were amongst the first recipients. *Cyrano de Bergerac* closed on March 22, 1947.

Joan of Arc was to be Ferrer's film debut. He had just arrived for his first visit to Cali-

Theda Bara, c. 1910. Sarony, New York (Stout Collection).

fornia from New York City. The Danneskjolds' guest quarters were to be Ferrer's home away from home.

After dinner, everyone adjourned to the living room. Maxwell Anderson sat at the grand piano and played a medley of his songs. Walter Wanger spoke about the founding of Sierra Pictures and thanked the Danneskjolds for their financial help and other supportive contributions. He then introduced his partners, Fleming and Bergman. Fleming announced that the filming of the production was to start on September 15th.

Jose Ferrer stood to recite a scene from *Cyrano de Bergerac*. Bergman, standing next to Anderson at the piano, then sang the lyrics to *September Song*, composed by Anderson. As Bergman sang the words, "Well, it's a long, long time from May to December, but the days grow short when you reach December," she stared directly into Mr. Fleming's eyes. She sang with a voice that was enchantingly beautiful and romantic.

As Mr. Fleming watched the artists now assembled together for the first time to recreate the legendary story of Joan of Arc, tears began to stream down his face. There was an emotional, breathtaking moment of silence before everyone applauded. After champagne was served, Theda graciously acknowledged everyone in the room, and as I stood next to her, she said, "We wouldn't all be here tonight if it weren't for this little child Joan who is so dear to me."

A Crashed Flying Disc

On the afternoon of Friday, July 4, 1947, my mother and I rode up a mountainous road to Lake Arrowhead, about an hour and a half's drive northeast of Los Angeles. Soon we were driving around the lake and I could see fireworks across the lake. We then entered through a guarded gate to the North Shore Tavern, owned by the Los Angeles Turf Club. This was an exclusive resort often frequented by celebrities. The main lodge and nine guest cottages were secluded in a forest within walking distance of the lake shore. The Brabins were staying at a nearby lodge. Upon arrival, they were greeted by Adolphe Menjou.

Upon registering, the guests were advised that there was only one seating for meals and you had to be there on time. Telephone service was not available; however, guests could receive or send messages from the Western Union Telex.

The next evening we stood in line with the heads of seven motion picture studios until the dining room doors were opened. The attire was dressy and the linen-covered tables held candles and flowers. We sat at a table with Congressman and Mrs. Richard Nixon. At the end of the dinner, the president of the Screen Actors Guild, Ronald Reagan, stood at the podium. He spoke about the concerns of members within the various organizations that had different political views. He concluded by saying, "Everyone in this room has a job to do." Reagan then turned the meeting over to the newly appointed chairman of HUAC, J. Parnell Thomas.

While staying at the resort, it was arranged for me to take tennis lessons with Bruno, a tennis coach from Peru. Bruno put me into a group session with actor Paul Henreid's daughters, Monica and Mimi. The Henreids had a Chris-Craft "Woody" speedboat and I learned to water ski behind it.

On July 8, 1947, posted at the front desk on a teletype message was the news that a crashed flying disc had been recovered from a ranch near Roswell, New Mexico. Everyone was quite concerned. We were told not to turn on any electric lights and someone passed out candles. All of the children were taken to Jack Chertok's house; Jack was the creator of *The Lone Ranger* and, later, *My Favorite Martian*. Their house was like a lodge, with a large family room which sported a pool table. We slept in sleeping bags. The next day it was reported that the debris was a weather balloon. I was sent back to the resort and everyone departed.

Finishing the Script

We returned to North Shore Tavern on the following Labor Day weekend. The Danneskjolds, Victor Fleming, Ingrid Bergman, the Brabins, Andrew Solt, Maxwell Anderson, and Jean Hersholt were there to finalize the script. Bergman had her own views regarding the script, and she let them be known. Hersholt, as an intermediary, was able to communicate with Bergman in her native language.

The concerns of censorship had constantly plagued the writers, so much so that each sentence of the script had to be closely scrutinized. There was major concern about the historical declarations of Joan of Arc: when she states that "her voices had deceived her," and at the trial when Joan declares that "her voices came from God and had not deceived her." Most certainly the clergy could not be turned into villains! There were discussions regarding removing the voices entirely, because the final script had to be approved by the National Legion of Decency. Theda herself was no stranger to censorship, especially from the church. The 1916 release of her film *The Serpent* raised eyebrows in her own hometown. Finally, the Catholic Federation of Cincinnati rejected the showing of the film in her hometown, which infuriated Theda.

Theda with her Russian Wolfhound, 1917 (Stout Collection).

As we stood in line waiting for the dining room to open, Hersholt spoke with Count Danneskjold concerning the tedious nature of his work and the difficulties in translating Hans Christian Andersen's *Fairy Tales* into English. Count Danneskjold agreed to help Hersholt with the translations, some of which he had learned as a child. Hersholt completed the Danish translations into English in 1949, entitling the book *The Complete Andersen*. It was a whopping six volumes which earned him the honor of being knighted by King Christian X of Denmark. Today the Danish actor and translator is honored by the Academy of Motion Picture Arts and Sciences by their presentation of the Jean Hersholt Humanitarian Award. This award goes to an actor whose humanitarian efforts have brought great honor to the film industry.

Hersholt concluded the evening by talking about his experience in the role of Shirley Temple's grandfather in the original movie *Heidi*, directed by Allen Dwan. Jean Hersholt was serving as president of the Academy of Motion Picture Arts and Sciences at that time. He concluded by reminding everyone about the importance of cooperating with HUAC.

September

Just before *Joan of Arc* filming began in September, the arrangement for its distribution by MGM was called off. Walter Wanger quickly secured distribution with RKO. In September of 1947, HUAC announced plans to hold hearings to determine the extent of Communist infiltration into the motion picture industry. It was almost a miracle that Victor Fleming was able to start filming on September 16th, Wanger announced that the film would not be released until the latter part of 1948.

On November 24, 1947, forty-eight Hollywood studio executives, along with their attorneys, met in secret at the Waldorf-Astoria Hotel in New York City to adopt a policy of procedure regarding the charges made by HUAC. This policy attempted to distance the executives from the "Hollywood Ten," stating that they would drop them from their employment rolls and not hire them until they had spoken in front of Congress to clear their names. However, the group also stated that in the current atmosphere, there was a danger of "hurting" innocent people and they would not engage in the hysteria of witch hunts. The letter was signed by Donald M. Nelson, president of the Society of Independent Motion Picture Producers.

Joan of Arc at the Stake

Uncle Charlie and Theda went to see most of the actual filming of *Joan of Arc* in the fall of 1947. Uncle Charlie would take his director's chair, some golf chairs that could be carried like an umbrella, and a pad and pencil to make notes. Theda contributed suggestions concerning the costumes, and Uncle Charlie contributed historical information when Maxwell Anderson needed it. They immensely enjoyed being a part of the process. Rex Tellegen worked as a runner, bringing sodas, helping with the props and parking cars.

I went to the filming both at the ranch and at the Hal Roach Studio. There were lots of people there for the scene where Ingrid Bergman is tied to a stake to be burned. In fact, there were so many people standing around, one could hardly see the event. Theda brushed my face with a little makeup. I was told to go over to the bales of hay and join the group of extras that surrounded Joan of Arc as she was being chained to the stake. When Mr. Fleming said, "Action," everyone reacted.

A Television Party

Theda liked to listen to the fights on the radio. She would get excited while listening to these broadcasts. The Brabins were the first to arrive at our house to watch the first broadcast on November 11, 1947, of Gorgeous George, the most flamboyant and entertaining wrestler at that time. John Tackaberry arrived with comedian Larry Parks, who added more humor to the TV broadcast viewing. Theda was very intrigued with Gorgeous George's blonde hair and his unusual sparkling costumes. She roared with laughter at his antics and thought that his show was the greatest.

Theda, a connoisseur of style, offers suggestions on the costumes to be used in *Joan of Arc* **(Stout Collection)**.

Soon after, I was looking out the window and lo and behold, there was Gorgeous George with his wife Betty knocking on Theda's front door! I quickly appeared with them at the door. After everyone was greeted and seated in the living room, I watched while Theda, using her mannequin, pointed to the neck and shoulders, giving helpful advice to Gorgeous George for his flamboyant costumes. He was so appreciative that he provided front row seats for Uncle Charlie, Theda and me at his next fight!

158th Infantry Regiment

Theda received a letter in December advising her that the 158th Infantry Regiment at Fort Tuthill, Arizona, for reasons due to restructuring after the war, was disbanding. (The unit had adopted Theda as

Theda Bara accepts the role of "Godmother of the 158th Infantry Regiment," June 1918 (Stout Collection).

its godmother in 1918.) The insignia for the infantry had been the coiled Bushmaster snake with a sword in the middle. It was the first Army unit to be trained in jungle warfare and the first Army unit to be sent overseas after Pearl Harbor. On December 17, 1947, its 102-year history ended with a ceremony on the football field at Phoenix Junior College. Theda stood for the last time as godmother of the regiment, as the "Bushmaster's 158th" passed for review. It was a fitting end for the regiment, and a sure sign of America in transition.

6

Friends for Life

1948

Not only was television on the horizon for the American household, long playing and single 45 records would soon be available. Show business was finally willing to open up to a wider audience via the new medium. Harold Adamson, who lived next door, would soon write the opening song for the *I Love Lucy* show. Columbia Records introduced the first 33⅓ RPM recording, "Christmas Songs by Sinatra." Buddy De Sylva, a co-founder of Capital Records, was full of excitement about the future of vinyl, stating, "Records are going to be a big business."

This was also a year that people were afraid that they might be socializing with a Communist, and for this reason many children were being home schooled, including myself. One of my school friends, Penny Diehl, remained at home because she was very sick with cystic fibrosis. When I told Theda about my friend, she found a way to have Penny come to the Brabin house for a visit.

Marionettes

Theda placed in the lanai, a movable stage with a large old marionette theater, complete with a curtain. She hung her childhood marionettes on chairs and placed the puppets on the seats. They were the most unusual puppets, all hand-carved out of wood. Each had an array of costumes. Some of the characters included Pinocchio and his cohorts, the Fairy with the Turquoise Hair, and the Ghost of the Talking Cricket. Also included were Hansel and Gretel, a Witch with a Broom,

Joan Craig (left) with friends: facing front, Geraldine Chaplin and Liza Minnelli (photograph provided by Joan Craig).

Harlequin, Villain, and Punch and Judy. Theda said, "The admission fare to see the puppet show is three gold coins." I wanted my friend Penny to see the play so I had to earn six gold chocolate coins by performing chores and helping neighbors. I quickly earned the six chocolate gold coins to pay for our admission.

Uncle Charlie served as the narrator, while Theda, Lori Bara and Mae Murray were the puppeteers. They performed "Jack and the Beanstalk," "Hansel and Gretel," and "Pinocchio." They had so much fun performing with the puppets that they took the act, along with the puppets and the stage, to the Los Angeles Children's Hospital for several performances.

The Metropolitan Opera

In April 1948, the Metropolitan Opera opened in Los Angeles for its first appearance there in forty-two years. Theda and Uncle Charlie took me to the opening night performance of *Carmen* at the Shrine Auditorium.

When we arrived, searchlights were sweeping back and forth across the sky. There were so many floodlights that the night was lit

6. Friends for Life

up like daylight! As we approached the auditorium, there was a long red carpet runway with fans alongside in bleachers to watch the arrival of the stars. As we walked across the red carpet, fans came running to get an autograph from Theda. As we entered, we were escorted to our seats several rows back from the stage in the middle of the auditorium. Friends of Theda and Uncle Charlie were seated all around us. Uncle Charlie told me the story of Carmen so that I could understand the performance. At the end, everyone cheered and there was vigorous applause. It was a very exciting evening. We were then ushered backstage to the dressing rooms to greet Nadine Conner, who played the leading role of the gypsy. Theda had played this part in Raoul Walsh's 1915 film version of *Carmen*.

Adoption

I soon decided that life was better across the street. I told Theda and Uncle Charlie that my sweet mother was not the person that they thought she was! I said, "My mother goes to luncheons every day and to Saks Fifth Avenue to have her hair done. When she takes me with her, she often forgets that I am there. When she arrives back home she wonders where I am. I often wait until the store closes and she is nowhere to be found."

Uncle Charlie said, "Your mother doesn't mean to forget you. She is just a little absent-minded!" Theda said, "This is child abuse!" I asked,

Theda Bara, 1918 (Stout Collection).

Theda Bara as Carolyn Knollys in *The Unchastened Woman*, 1925 (Stout Collection).

"Can I live with you? I won't cost much. I can go across the street and get my dinner."

Uncle Charlie and Theda thought this over quite seriously. They sent a message to my parents that they would like to adopt me. My parents' response was that I could not go over there for awhile.

Canasta

I taught Theda how to play canasta. She liked the game so much that she came over to our house every week to a canasta party. One of the ladies who often came to play was Mary Adams Balmat from Deadwood, North Dakota. Her life had become something of a scandal in the town because of her marriage to a man who was more than forty years her senior. Mary stated that her elder suitor sent her a room full of roses every Saturday and that was the reason she accepted his proposal of marriage.

My grandmother, Helen Craven LaTourette, the third player, was born in 1869. She was from an era when women cinched their waists with a corset until they could hardly breathe! She wore a corset that had to be tightened every day with strings, and this was the case even on her 101st birthday. She had been a tennis and golf champion in her day, a sportswoman at a time when it was considered unacceptable for ladies to play those games.

Joan with her mother, Helen "Betty" Craig (photograph provided by Joan Craig).

The fourth player, Bess Cregar, was the mother of Laird Cregar, an actor who was known in Hollywood as the "hulky villain." Bess had become a widow with six children shortly after Laird was born. Bess's husband, Edward, had been a member and manager of the first world tour cricket team, known as the "Gentlemen of Philadelphia" in the 1890s. Bess had an engaging subtle humor that Theda particularly enjoyed.

These rebelliously strong-willed women liked the challenge of the game; none of them wanted to be the loser! They were so attentive to the game that Theda said to me, "Now when you go through the room, don't say a word. I know you are there." Sometimes I would hear one of the ladies make a remark or tell a joke to distract the other players. When Mary lost a game, she would entice the others to continue playing another round until she won!

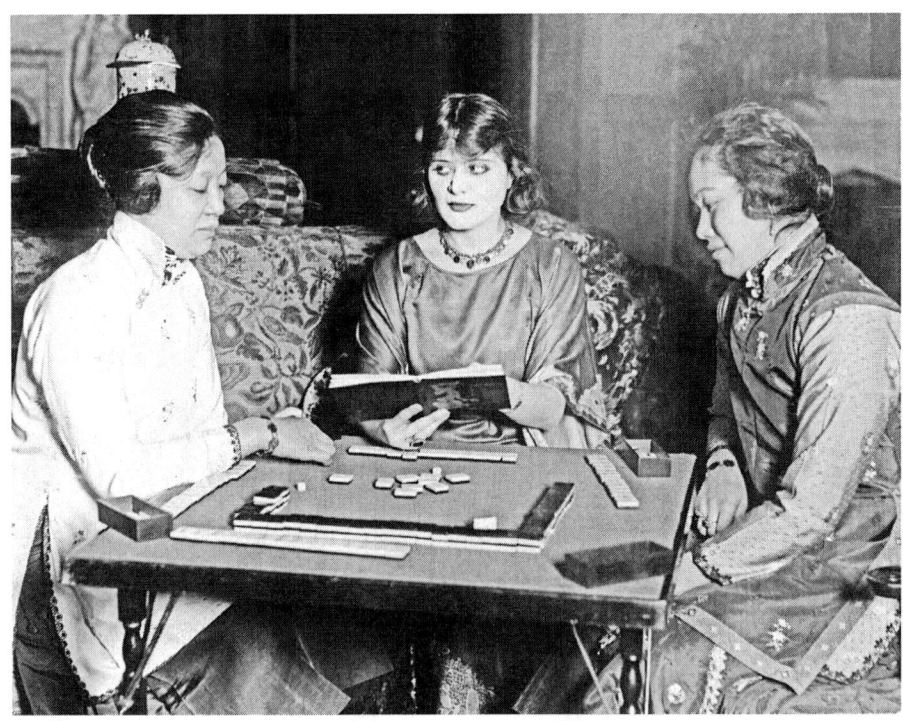

Theda plays the game Pung Chow at the Westchester Biltmore Club. Two Chinese ladies instruct her in this Royal Game of China. December 7, 1922 (Stout Collection).

The Premiere of Joan of Arc

Just before Christmas 1948, the long-awaited *Joan of Arc* opened at the Beverly Theater on the corner of Beverly Drive and Wilshire Boulevard in Beverly Hills. Seating capacity at the Beverly was smaller than most other movie theaters at the time. When Uncle Charlie, Theda and I arrived, there was a red carpet rolled all the way out to the curb. We were greeted by Walter Wanger and Victor Fleming. Victor said, "She's late!" as he anxiously awaited Ingrid Bergman's arrival. Victor was shocked to see that Bergman's new boyfriend, director Roberto Rossellini, also arrived for the premiere. Theda and Charles had recognized him standing in front of the theater at the side. Victor said, "I'm going in." Bergman finally made her entrance and stood in the theater aisle until someone gave up their seat. There were two intermissions and at the first intermission some people left. By the time the second intermission started, some guests were overheard saying, "This is Bergman's Joan, not Victor Fleming's." At the end of the film there was a long moment of silence. Mary Pickford was sitting several rows in front of us and all of a sudden she stood up and applauded.

Joan of Arc won the Academy Award for Best Cinematography and Best Costume Design for 1948. It was the first film to receive seven Academy Award nominations without receiving a Best Picture nomination.

Theda Bara, c. 1918 (Stout Collection).

Hollywood Loses Fleming

In 1949, Victor Fleming died on January 6, the accepted day for the birthday of Joan of Arc. He died while vacationing with his family in Cottonwood, Arizona. He was 59 years old.

Fleming directed many films during his career, chief among them *Gone with the Wind*, *The Wizard of Oz*, *Dr. Jekyll and Mr. Hyde*, and *Captains Courageous*. He is recognized as one of Hollywood's greatest filmmakers.

Theda, Uncle Charlie and I attended the funeral held at St. Alban's Church in Westwood. The church was so full of people that some had to stand in the back. Tears streamed down my face during the whole service. I can't help but say that I had a crush on him. I could hear Clark Gable sobbing loudly. He had lost his closest friend. Victor Fleming was a very special friend to us and many, many people in the Hollywood community. He was direct, and he expected the best from his cast and crew. He inspired creativity and captured the best of every actor with whom he worked.

You Have the Best Part

Our French class at school was going to perform a play completely in French. The setting was to be a French market with shoppers. Our teacher, Madam Egan, gave me a script but I didn't have any lines. I was very upset. My friend Ava was going to be the narrator. Theda, with a very concerned look on her face, asked, "Who made the decision that you weren't to have

Theda Bara, c. 1918 (Stout Collection).

6. Friends for Life

a speaking part?" I told her that during our French studies, a glass full of ice cream sticks with names on each one was passed around. Each student drew a stick that awarded a part.

At first Theda thought that this had something to do with her but then she exclaimed, "You got the best part." I was to be a little orphan girl who cleaned around the marketplace. Theda rehearsed with me. She explained to me that when someone came on stage that I should react.

Theda decided that my costume should be made of black silk with a black beret. She measured me and made a pattern for a silk button-down jacket with long sleeves and black silk pants. She made the whole costume including the beret.

Theda told me to cover the stage with the broom. She said, "While doing so, you can pick up an apple or an orange and look at it. You can sweep and put your hands on your hips and make faces. The stage is yours; you have the best part!" However, at rehearsal, Madam Egan didn't like my antics. She said that I was to stand in the corner of the stage and sweep the floor.

The Westlake School for Girls puts on a French play. Seated far left is Joan Craig. The narrator under the umbrella is her childhood friend, Ava Astaire. Theda made the costume Joan is wearing, c. 1949 (photograph by Hap Byers, photographer).

The moment came when Theda entered the auditorium wearing a hat and a black veil. She seated herself in the middle with Uncle Charlie next to her. The auditorium was full and many celebrities were in attendance. People turned and whispered, "Do you see who is here? What is she doing here?" They were referring to Theda, the star.

Before the curtain was raised, my friend Ava began to narrate the story. She spoke clearly to the audience and without a hint of nervousness in her voice. At that moment, I decided that I was not going to stay in the corner with the broom! The curtain was raised and I began to sweep the whole stage. The shoppers came to the market. By doing the little actions that Theda had taught me, there was never a dull moment. Before the class took their bow, I took my bow the way that Theda had shown me. The audience laughed heartily!

Finding Montgomery Clift

One afternoon, director George Stevens came to the Brabin house for dinner. He brought with him the film *The Search* to run after dinner. Montgomery Clift had won a Best Actor nomination for his performance as Ralph Stevenson, an American G.I. in post–World War II Germany.

After viewing the film, Stevens remarked that he was very impressed with Clift; however, he felt that Clift was vulnerable to Hollywood influences. Stevens then told Theda and Uncle Charlie that he wanted to present his script, *A Place in the Sun*, to Clift for consideration. He went on to explain how he and Clift had the same agent, Charles K. Feldman. Having the same agent was often a way to collaborate on projects; however, Stevens felt that Feldman also had the power to blow this particular deal. He asked the Brabins for help.

A luncheon was arranged in the commissary at Paramount Studios. The commissary was in a building that had an elevator that took patrons almost to the basement where there was a dining room without windows. "Monty" Clift escorted us to a table. He quickly explained that he was serving as host for the dining room that day and that he would have to seat people when they came in.

Clift had already achieved fame in *Red River* and *The Search*. Sets were being built for his next film, Paramount's *The Heiress*. Monty said, "Everyone knows that I am here so that I can be found. You're only as good as your last film, so I work here so that I can save my money."

6. Friends for Life

Uncle Charlie was not surprised and immediately said that he had the same concerns when he worked at Edison Films in New Jersey.

Monty was soft-spoken and gracious in manner. He welcomed Theda with great respect. He never thought that he would have the

Theda in an early pose, c. 1919. Underwood and Underwood Studios, New York (Stout Collection).

opportunity to meet the world-renowned actress. He seemed a little apprehensive as to why we were there. It took a long time before the lunch was served.

Uncle Charlie handed the script for *A Place in the Sun* to Monty while explaining that it was adapted from the novel *An American Tragedy* by Theodore Dreiser. Monty said that he had received many scripts. He then said, "I'm an actor and when I look at a script, I am looking for a role that requires acting. It doesn't necessarily need to be a lead role. And I want to be very careful and not get tied up with a studio contract." Uncle Charlie assured him that a studio contract would not be required; however, he requested that Clift not delay in looking over the script.

Monty seemed to relax as the conversations turned to other topics. Theda asked him if he had been to see the beautiful expansive gardens at the Huntington Library in Pasadena. Monty's face brightened and he said that he enjoyed museums and then stated that he would like to see the gardens. Theda extended an invitation for Monty to join us for a picnic lunch at the Huntington Library.

During the filming of *The Heiress*, my mother drove Theda and Uncle Charlie to at least a dozen picnics with Monty in the Huntington Gardens. Everyone enjoyed the picnics in the lush garden setting. Uncle Charlie and Monty would go on long walks together. I would sometimes see them off in the distance. It looked like Monty was describing a scene. I don't think the two of them ever stopped talking. Monty made some script changes and when Uncle Charlie said that he liked them, Monty finally agreed to sign a contract for *A Place in the Sun*.

Stevens wanted Elizabeth Taylor for the female lead. On August 9, 1949, *The New York Times* reported that Taylor was temporarily withdrawn from the cast of *Father of the Bride*. MGM had loaned Taylor to Paramount to star in *A Place in the Sun*.

Father of the Bride, starring Taylor, Joan Bennett and Spencer Tracy, was filmed at All Saints Episcopal Church in Beverly Hills. The film was directed by Vincente Minnelli, then-husband of Judy Garland. During the filming at the church, Uncle Charlie and Theda were there to keep track of props. The filming seemed like a "family and friends" affair, with several of Theda's close pals on the set. Theda gave a dinner party with Taylor and Nicky Hilton Jr. as the honored guests. The buffet of roast beef and Yorkshire pudding, Theda's steak and kidney pie, and the lamb mousse was an absolute feast. Elizabeth gave her book *Nibbles and Me* to Theda to give to me.

The Pageant of the Masters

In the summer of 1949 we went to see the Pageant of the Masters in Laguna Beach. The pageant presented a series of famous artworks with live characters in detailed sets. This was to be a special evening for Theda. We were allowed entry before the crowd arrived and we met with the director of the pageant. That year a Norman Rockwell painting was featured. Theda, an admirer of Rockwell, greeted him at the entrance to the theater. As I watched the performance, I was amazed at how still the actors stood. I could not visualize that they were even alive! As we watched, I could feel Theda's passion for the theater. Theda expressed how difficult it was to stay perfectly still in a pose for a long period of time. Uncle Charlie spoke of the importance of precise measurements when creating the sets. It was necessary to make both the actors and the sets appear exactly as the painting appeared.

Theda's Life Story

In February of 1949, Buddy De Sylva arranged a working luncheon with Theda and Uncle Charlie at the Formosa Café in Hollywood to discuss producing a film based on Theda's life. It was to be shot on the Paramount lot. De Sylva had chosen Betty Hutton to play Theda. He was very excited because he had with him the contracts for the movie. Betty expressed that she was honored to be chosen for the film. Buddy commented on her box office popularity.

Hutton was dressed in a sleek pair of slacks, accompanied by a suede jacket and blouse. She wore very little makeup. She made notes and seemed to be very businesslike with a perky, positive attitude. I didn't perceive her as being a movie star. I couldn't see any resemblance to Theda. However, as I sat and listened to the conversation, I realized that resemblance wasn't as important as one's acting ability. After all, resemblance could be achieved in makeup and wardrobe. It was a surprise to me that everyone remarked about my likeness to Betty Hutton!

Buddy mentioned that as the partner of music store owner Glenn Wallich and lyricist and songwriter Johnny Mercer, his small investment with Columbia Records was soaring in value. He went on to explain that writing songs was a hobby that he enjoyed and that he had in mind some songs for the movie. Buddy had written such hits as "April Showers," "California Here I Come," "The Best Things in Life Are Free," and "Sunny Side Up." (He was posthumously inducted into the Songwriter's Hall of Fame in 1970.) It was nearly dinner time when we departed.

On Location with Cleopatra

Buddy De Sylva wanted to see the location where Fox had filmed the sea and land battles for Theda's 1917 blockbuster, *Cleopatra*. We drove to Balboa Island in Newport Bay where De Sylva joined us for burgers at the famous Jolly Roger Restaurant on the island. We then walked across a bridge to what is known as Little Island. At that time, Balboa Island consisted of large stretches of sand bars without any structures. It was known for its beautiful view of the narrow waterways, shoreline cliffs, and white sandy beaches.

On the set of *Cleopatra*, 1917 (Stout Collection).

6. Friends for Life

As I listened to the conversation, Theda described the area as the location for the sea Battle of Actium. In ancient Egyptian times, the war pitted Octavian and his Roman army against the combined forces of Antony's men and the Egyptian army, led by Cleopatra. According to Theda, J. Gordon Edwards had assembled on Little Island nearly a thousand extras dressed in Nubian, Egyptian, and Roman costumes. She said that Edwards was able to film the battle in one day.

She said that the warriors carried realistic weapons. She also stated that most of the extras did not know how to swim. Therefore, nearby fishermen were cast for overboard shots.

Uncle Charlie spoke of the twenty-nine floating barges that were used to create full-scale replicas of the Roman galleons. Each galley ship was manned by sixty oarsmen. Cleopatra's galley was very elaborate.

We walked to several places on Little Island where we could see Balboa while Uncle Charlie described the filming of *Cleopatra*. He pointed to the narrow waterway between Little Island and the larger Balboa Island as a location for the close-up shots of the battle. Uncle Charlie had brought with him a portfolio of photographs (taken in August of 1917) of the ships, actors, and their encampment.

As we walked to the shore facing the mainland, Uncle Charlie described the re-enactment of the Roman naval attack on Cleopatra's Egyptian forces. This location was where twenty-nine galley ships had followed Theda's command galley. Edwards supervised forty-five cameras, all rolling at once on every angle of the battle scene. The scene was of such magnitude that there was much destruction to the ships and props. This was the main reason that the battle had to be filmed in one take.

Theda remarked that the scenes were very dangerous because they were hurling huge fire balls at the fleets. Some of the fireballs would land where the actors were standing. The ships became engulfed in flames and then sank under the waves. As in most accounts of history, all the ships were set afire and destroyed except for Cleopatra's galley, which had turned and fled for Egypt.

During the filming, Balboa Island had become a sea of tents which housed the actors and crew members. Hundreds of people from the area stood on the mainland bluff that day to watch from a distance the filming of the battle.

Later we drove to the cliffs of Rocky Point which were near the ocean channels of Newport Bay. Theda told us that Cleopatra's galley was finally crushed to splinters on the beach just below Rocky Point during the filming.

The *Newport News* called the filming "the most magnificent and spectacular scene ever taken on water." The story was picked up and reported by the *Los Angeles Times* on August 16, 1917. The article stated, "Bara spent her time in Newport Beach exploring the local beaches and Newport harbor during the filming." Theda was quoted in the *Times* as saying, "I enjoyed Balboa hugely, and I used to delight in hiring a rowboat by night and skimming the bay."

The *Times* also reported that Theda's boat was almost capsized by another small boat, which was piloted by two young local boys. One of the boys recognized Theda by the light of his lantern; it was reported that he had watched the stars as they filmed the battle.

Another night, Theda visited a rocky point at Newport Beach to read by the moonlight. However, as she read, the tide came in. Theda stated, "Before I knew it, the

Theda Bara as Cleopatra, from the 1917 film *Cleopatra* (Stout Collection).

Theda as Cleopatra (Stout Collection).

strip of beach on which I had come over was covered by water. I had to climb a nearly perpendicular rock to reach the mainland and even then I was very nearly marooned." She went on to say that "in another hour I should have been entirely cut off from land!"

Contract Signed

There were many meetings between Buddy DeSylva and Theda regarding a film based on her life story. A decision was made that I would portray Theda as a young child in the film, entitled "The Great Vampire." Betty Hutton had agreed to portray Theda as an adult. Upon delivering my signed contract to Buddy DeSylva at his office above Wallach's Music City in Hollywood, Mr. DeSylva gave me the album "Goldilocks and the Three Bears," narrated by Margaret O'Brien. As I listened to O'Brien's beautifully spoken words, I felt certain that I did not have the talent to be a child actress. I proceeded to devote my interest to rocks and gemstones. I told all concerned that I wanted to be a gemologist!

Sadly, the story would not go forward. Buddy De Sylva died suddenly of a heart attack on July 11, 1950. Theda mourned the loss of Buddy, her friend. She also realized that all of the high hopes for a biopic were now only whispery shadows. She believed that this loss was karma and in the future no one would remember her. By this time, Theda was aware that most of her films had not survived. And now the story of her life would never be filmed. Uncle Charlie said to her, "Moody, you will always be remembered as 'The Vamp.'"

Stock Market on the Rise

The stock market was on a rise in the first half of the 1950s. Uncle Charlie had a file cabinet in his room full of stock and bond certificates. With a Standard & Poors Blue Book that he gave me to use, I helped him research the value of each certificate. It took months to trace and research each certificate by its number. Some of the stocks were in the thousands of shares. I learned about the stock ratings. The companies that I researched were mostly A-rated at the time the stocks were purchased. Many were utility company stocks. It was a shock to Uncle Charlie and me to learn that none of the certificates had any value due to the 1929 stock market crash and the Depression.

Uncle Charlie was very sad thinking about the disappointments and losses that he had during his life. He would have been a very wealthy man even if each share was worth only one dollar. Uncle Charlie taught me how to chart the weekly price quotes from the newspaper. He encouraged me to invest. I called my father's stockbroker and purchased four shares of Decca Records at four dollars a share. Uncle Charlie said, "It is just as important to decide when to sell as it is to

Theda Bara, c. 1919, Campbell Studios, New York (Stout Collection).

decide to buy a stock." My goal was to buy a bicycle. The stock price on the Decca shares rose quickly. My sixteen dollar investment enabled me to purchase a bicycle several months later.

Ambassador to Luxembourg

On June 3, 1951, Theda and Uncle Charlie gave a dinner party for Perle Mesta, the American socialite and political hostess. Perle gave very lavish parties and was known as "the hostess with the mostest." She was also appointed as the first American Minister to Luxembourg by President Truman in 1949. She served in this capacity until 1953.

An Oklahoma City girl, Perle was the daughter of oil man Bill Skirvin, owner of the lavish Skirvin Towers Hotel in Oklahoma City. She was widowed from steel tycoon George Mesta after nearly five years of marriage. With his death, she inherited his seventy-eight million dollar fortune. She became famous for bringing the right people together at the right time.

Charles Brabin, Theda Bara, Perle Mesta, Mr. and Mrs. Carl Hansen, June 3, 1951 (University of Southern California Digital Libraries).

After the guests arrived at the Brabins, they were free to wander through the house to the solarium and into the backyard where pole tents had been placed for the party. Theda had decorated the backyard with floral bouquets of red roses enhanced with baby's breath flowers. The party was the event of the year, bringing nearly a hundred of Hollywood's most powerful people together. Ronald Reagan, the Screen Actors Guild president, made an opening speech in which he introduced George Murphy as vice president of Technicolor and Desilu Studios. Ethel Merman sang "God Bless America" without accompaniment. As her powerful voice sang the phrase "Stand beside her, and guide her," I knew she meant it! I cannot help but think that on this day Ethel Merman inspired Reagan and Murphy on to their respective careers. George Murphy would go on to become the chairman of the California Republican State Central Committee later that year, and Ronald Reagan would go on to be elected president of the United States in 1980.

Merman then sang a medley of Irving Berlin's songs from the Broadway musical, *Call Me Madam*. She concluded with "There's No Business Like Show Business" from *Annie Get Your Gun*. The party was one that I will always remember.

7

Traveling Abroad

The Coronation

Theda and Uncle Charlie received a formal invitation to the Coronation of Queen Elizabeth II. It was a great honor to receive an invitation to the social event of the century. It read:

> *By Command of the Queen*
> *The Earl Marshall is directed to invite*
> *Sir Charles and Theda Bara Brabin*
> *To be present in the Abbey Church of St. Peter, Westminster*
> *On Tuesday, 2nd June, 1953*

This invitation was tearfully read to me by Theda. It was one of her happiest moments that I can remember. From the time that the invitation arrived, Uncle Charlie seemed to come alive. His smile was radiant and he seemed to be well in spirit. Both he and Theda were humbled by the invitation. It was a great honor to be invited to the coronation. The invitation was also an acknowledgment by the monarchy that Charles and Theda had both risen to the top of their respective fields.

My parents helped make the arrangements for the Brabins to travel on a special voyage of the SS *President Roosevelt* which was scheduled to dock in Southampton, England, in time for the event. Also on board were beautiful orchid floral arrangements from Sam Mosher's Dos Pueblos Orchid Company of Goleta, California, for the reception dinner at Buckingham Palace.

On sailing day we drove Theda and Uncle Charlie to the Port of Long Beach. There were bands playing and my family and I were able to board for a small party in their stateroom. As the ship sailed out of port with its horn blowing, everyone threw streamers from the dock.

Theda as Lisza in *The Rose of Blood*, 1917 (Stout Collection).

It was pouring rain and the skies were dismal gray in England on Coronation Day. The women, in beautiful long gowns, could not avoid being soaked by the cloudbursts. The guests proceeded into the long entrance to Westminster Abby, past the statues of heraldic symbols known as the Queen's Beasts. Everyone had to be seated before eight

7. Traveling Abroad

A.M. Theda and Uncle Charlie had been provided an Abbey seat number with their invitation. They were seated near the aisle on the right hand side where they had a full view of the queen's procession. The event started promptly at eleven. The guests were not allowed to leave until the ceremony and the related formalities concluded at three.

On the day of the coronation, my mother and I flew from Los Angeles to London. Thursday morning we joined Uncle Charlie and Theda for breakfast at the Claridge's Mayfair Hotel. My mother's duties were to oversee the flower arrangements sent from Dos Pueblos Orchid Ranch to Buckingham Palace for the reception dinners to be held Thursday and Friday, June 4 and 5.

The orchid growers, located in Santa Barbara's coastal region, had originally purchased cymbidiums from England. It was discovered that the region's climate and sandy soils provided the necessary setting for the flowers to grow and flourish. Oil tycoon Sam Mosher had assembled one of the best orchid breeding collections in the world, with flowers from all over the globe. Throughout the 1950s and '60s, the Dos Pueblos Orchid Company was the largest orchid producer in the world, with some two millions plants in its inventory.

After breakfast, my mother and I went to Buckingham Palace. We entered into the Grand Hall and were escorted up the curving marble stairs for a quick tour of the rooms that would be used for the banquet. We were then directed to the Royal Mews. While passing through to a room where the floral arrangements were stored, I was able to see the ornate hand-painted gold carriage that was used to transport Queen Elizabeth II during the coronation.

The floral bouquets were placed in tall vases. There was a tiered array of Birds of Paradise, other exotic flowers with vivid colors, and the most beautiful orchids. The arrangements were brought into Buckingham Palace and placed on each table to serve as a centerpiece.

On the day of the reception we arrived early. My mother tended to the last-minute details of the table arrangements. The Royal Family assembled for the receiving line to greet their guests at the coronation dinner. It was breathtaking to see the queen in all her glory! The notable attendees were dressed in the most unusual and elegant attire. Some of the guests were dressed in their country's traditional diplomatic attire.

All guests were assigned to a banquet room. There were name cards at each table. My mother and I waited until most of the guests had arrived to proceed through the receiving line to the Throne Room.

It was in this room that I was introduced to Prime Minister Winston Churchill. Uncle Charlie and Theda were seated at a table near the center of the White Drawing Room for the eight-course formal candlelight dinner.

Her Majesty, Queen Elizabeth II, appeared at the doorway wearing her beautiful white coronation dress. She entered the White Drawing Room and stood in the center to greet her guests. She asked for each person to introduce themselves by giving their name and the name of their country.

The queen introduced Theda Bara as an honored guest. She spoke about the Globe Theatre in which Shakespeare worked and wrote many of his great plays. Theda's career encompassed Shakespeare's works in her silent films. The queen stated that her father, King George VI, admired Theda's accurate portrayal of Juliet in Fox's 1916 film *Romeo and Juliet*.

St. Donat's Castle, Wales

The Brabins' itinerary included staying several nights at the Claridge's Mayfair Hotel in London, and then an overnight ferry ride from Dover to Calais for a weekend stay in Paris with friends. Also planned was a visit with Marion Davies at St. Donat's Castle at Glamorgan, on the south coast of Wales.

William Randolph Hearst had purchased the castle in 1925 for Davies and had spent a fortune on renovations. These included the installation of electricity in the castle and improvements to the surrounding area. St. Donat's Castle was known to be the most haunted castle in Wales. It was also known as the castle with the most beautiful views of the sea.

Davies had returned with her husband, Captain Horace Brown, to St. Donat's to oversee the repairs. The documents for the sale of the castle to an anonymous buyer arrived by courier while I was there.

Davies, with her lively personality, thrived on entertaining guests. By the time I arrived, she, Theda and Uncle Charlie were ready to entertain me. Marion and Theda led me on a tour while telling me the tale of an exorcism that succeeded in ridding the castle of its apparitions. I was told that a hag and a mysterious yellow eye had appeared on the ceilings of several rooms and that I should look for the Black Panther!

7. Traveling Abroad

Theda was most anxious to go into the rooms where apparitions had appeared. We each carried a glass of water as we proceeded down a corridor past more than thirty-five bedrooms to the original guest rooms. Theda placed a glass of water down and said, "If the water shakes or ripples, a ghost is amongst us." We then proceeded to an original part of the fifteenth century castle. We passed the priest's room and arrived at the Great Hall, where in 1738 candles had set fire to the motifs around the coffin of Sir Thomas. The flames got out of control and burned much of the castle. After the burial of Sir Thomas, the Stradling family ownership of St. Donat's Castle came to an end.

Uncle Charlie and Captain Brown kept the ladies entertained by telling jokes during the dinner courses. Marion responded by mimicking Mae Murray and other actors, making us laugh until we hurt! After dinner we adjourned to the drawing room. We then played charades.

Marion spoke of the happy times spent with William Hearst while rebuilding the castle. She told us about the collection of silver and the statues of armor that were no longer there. She also spoke about the times when Hearst lent the castle to the famous Welshman, Prime Minister David Lloyd George, also known as Chancellor of the Exchequer, and the first Lloyd George of Dwyfor, to entertain the Bards of the Eisteddfod. (The Eisteddfod was a Welsh festival of literature, music, and performance, dating back to the twelfth century.)

Trumpeters were on the castle walls and the Bards had to claim their admittance, to which Lloyd George, as lord of the manor, gave a reply. There were harpists and jesters, songs and poetry.

Marion's eyes were full of tears as she told of William Hearst's passing and the closing

Theda Bara with the Raven, 1916 (Stout Collection).

of the castle shortly after. She said, "We now shall say goodbye by giving our best performance to the ghosts of St. Donat's."

Down the darkened ghostly hallways of the castle we went, again carrying candles to light our way. Theda ran from room to room and opened every door so that Marion could sweep every room. Then up the staircase we went, to the drawing room and finally to the ballroom. Theda continued to open each door. We then went down the stairs to the breakfast room and on to Bradenstoke Hall. Marion swept until there were no more rooms to sweep. We then proceeded back to the great hall. The whole time we had proceeded through the castle, I was reciting "The Raven" by Edgar Allan Poe.

The Raven

Once upon a midnight dreary, while I pondered, weak and weary,
Over many a quaint and curious volume of forgotten lore—
While I nodded, nearly napping, suddenly there came a tapping,
As of someone gently rapping, rapping at my chamber door.
"'Tis some visitor," I muttered, "tapping at my chamber door—
Only this and nothing more." ...

We then proceeded into the Great Hall where the moonlight peered through. With a book in hand, I began to recite lines from *Romeo and Juliet* and *Macbeth*. As soon as I was finished, Theda stood before the fireplace and recited *The Vampire* by Rudyard Kipling. The title of Theda's first big film was the first four words of the poem:

The Vampire

A fool there was and he made his prayer
(Even as you and I!)
To a rag and a bone and a hank of hair
(We called her the woman who did not care),
But the fool he called her his lady fair
(Even as you and I!) ...

We continued our performance to honor the ghosts of St. Donat's. We each recited a part of Shakespeare's tragedy *Cymbeline*. The play recounts the legend of the early Celtic King Cunobelinus, with themes of innocence and jealousy throughout. The play was performed by a leading Shakespearean actress in Britain in the 1880s, Ellen Terry, whose work was well known to Theda, Charles and Marion.

At the close of the evening, just before midnight, we left all the doors open for the ghosts to roam freely until the morning light. In the morning, after closing all the doors, we gathered in the Beast Gar-

7. *Traveling Abroad* 95

Theda with her dog Momo, 1916 (Stout Collection).

den with the legendary mystical beasts. All the ghosts and memories had been set free. We each chose a beast and made a wish for St. Donat's Castle to be cared for and be available for future study by scholars.

The anonymous buyer's offer to purchase St. Donat's Castle was a standing offer to be transferred at a time of convenience. At this time, Marion Davies had inherited control of William Randolph Hearst's empire. During our visit, Davies had expressed that she was not desirous of Hearst's money and that she had made arrangements to return her rights as heir to Hearst's estate.

Kissing the Blarney Stone

Soon we traveled to Dublin for a stay at Lismore Castle, the former residence of Lord Charles Arthur Francis Cavendish and Fred Astaire's sister, Lady Charles Cavendish. Theda and Charles had invited seventy-five guests for lunch at Lismore Castle's banquet hall. Some of the guests had attended the queen's coronation reception. Theda had a longing desire to kiss the Blarney Stone. She wanted to receive the gift of eloquence. She also believed that the Blarney Stone was the stone of destiny and that it had great mystical powers.

The day before the luncheon we went to the village for lunch. While waiting for it to be served, I was left unattended for a few minutes. I then overheard a conversation: "When she kisses the Blarney Stone she will slip and fall, and when the little girl makes the announcement, she will go out the exit door and with a little push, she will fall down the cliff. The attention will be on the loss of the child." When I turned around to see who had spoken, no one was there!

Theda and Charles left for Blarney Castle early on the morning of the luncheon. Upon arriving, they ascended the stairs to the castle's peak. Uncle Charlie was first, and leaned backwards and kissed the Blarney Stone without any trouble. While Theda was leaning on her back with her head over the 600-foot drop, she reached for the rails with assistants holding her legs. She lost her grip with one rail and was unable to pull herself back up. Thank goodness the assistants were there! I was terribly upset at this turn of events considering the words I had overheard the day before!

In the banquet hall of Lismore Castle, all the guests were seated and waiting for Theda and Charles to appear. I was told to announce that there would be a short delay and to leave through the door below the exit sign. As I was finishing the announcement, Theda appeared on crutches with her leg bound in a cast. After the luncheon was served, everyone signed her cast. It was time for me to leave for the long return to Beverly Hills. Just to be cautious, I did not go out the exit door. Instead I returned to the hall where I had entered.

Theda and Charles returned to their home in Nova Scotia after the trip to Blarney Castle. After a short stay, they came back to the United States with a stopover at Theda's New York City residence in Gramercy Park. (It was said that Theda's Gramercy Park residence was kept just as she left it until well into the 1970s.)

7. *Traveling Abroad*

Upon their return to Beverly Hills, Theda and Uncle Charlie gave me souvenirs that they had acquired. I made a scrapbook out of the collection for them. It included the invitation to the coronation, the Great Seal of the Realm, four-leaf clovers from Ireland, ship luggage labels, postcards, and restaurant menus. One menu was from Tour d'Argent in the Eiffel Tower. I added maps of London, Paris, and Dublin, along with a story of their long journey. Later Uncle Charlie asked for my permission to send the book to the queen for her historical archives.

8

Back Home in Los Angeles

The Disney Dream

On September 12, 1953, Theda and Charles hosted an afternoon garden buffet party. Roy Disney and a gentleman from Disney Studio attended. One of them placed an easel with a big white pad of paper in Theda's dining room. On the paper was written a number with dollar signs and the printed word **Needed**! Another easel had an aerial photograph of orange groves in Anaheim, and on the table was a pencil sketch of Disney's "Main Street, USA." There was an attendance poll sheet attached to a clipboard with the questions, "Would you attend this park?" And "How many are in your family?"

Mary Balmat was very interested and thought that this was a wonderful idea. She decided to stay at the dining table with them and listen to the comments and questions as the men described Disney's dream to the guests. The most important statement made by Disney that afternoon was, "The park can open one year from ground break."

The next afternoon we went with Theda, Uncle Charlie and Mary to Walt Disney's home in nearby Holmby Hills. Mary wanted to personally hand a check to Walt Disney for the development of his dream park, Disneyland. Mary had inherited $100,000 in 1934 when her husband died, and she had invested the money wisely. She lived in a two-room apartment with a bed in a closet-sized room in Los Angeles. She preferred to give scholarships to young musicians first, and then spend some money on herself.

Mary's investment with Disney proved to be more than prudent. She formed the Adams-Mastrovich Family Foundation that became

8. Back Home in Los Angeles

Birthday party honoring Mary Adams Balmat. *Standing:* Carroll Henderson Hansen, Joan Craig, Anne Payton, Betty Craig. Seated: Joe Birdsall, Mary Adams Balmat (photograph provided by Joan Craig).

one of the largest donors for the building of the Los Angeles Philharmonic's Walt Disney Concert Hall designed by Frank Gehry.

As early as 1906, Charles Brabin impersonated Lincoln in *The Life of Lincoln* on stage. It was one of his most successful roles as an actor. One of Walt Disney's dreams was to have a theme attraction featuring Abraham Lincoln. Uncle Charlie contributed to the idea based on his previous performances as Lincoln. It became part of the development "Great Moments with Lincoln" which was first shown at the 1964 World's Fair in New York City. Later it was moved to Disneyland as a free attraction.

At Home

I joined a little play group and performed a monologue from *Joan of Arc*. The performances were held at various churches. Theda made my costume and before each performance she did my makeup. Max Factor pancake makeup was applied all over my face including my hairline. She used Maybelline cake mascara and a rabbit's foot to blend in the rouge on my cheeks. She then powdered my face and buffed my nails with powder to make them shine.

Theda emphasized the importance of removing all the makeup with Ponds Cream immediately after a performance. She showed me how she made her own makeup. Theda would grind small gemstone pieces using a mortar and pestle. She mixed the stone dust, henna, tal-

Charles and Theda Bara Brabin, 1923 (Stout Collection).

cum powder, and rosewater for eye shadow. Other items she mentioned were beeswax, royal bee jelly, and sandalwood.

Theda liked to design her own clothes. She would see something in a magazine and get an idea. Out would come a mannequin and scissors. I would go with her to shop for the material and sometimes we would take the mannequin and material in a taxi to the dressmaker. Theda also would design and make her own hats.

The wigs with real hair that were made for Theda's performances were made by her mother. Some of the wigs had waistline-length hair and some were hairpieces with curls. Theda's costumes were stored in the basement. She explained to me that she provided many of the costumes that she had worn in her films. In addition to the costumes, Theda also designed and made many of the headpieces. Uncle Charlie, always the historian, stressed the importance of period detail. One of the headdresses that was especially dear to Theda was the Falcon Crown. She spoke about the silk thread colors that she chose for the crown; they had a special meaning. This was the crown that was used in the film *Cleopatra* for her coronation ceremony.

Every once in a while Theda would place the ouija board on the table and we would sit with our fingers on the dial and watch it move from letter to letter. We would try to read the messages. The smell of incense would enhance the spirits. Theda's little black cat, Puddy, would curl up near us. Uncle Charlie would seem to magically appear with a rose from the garden for each of us. His disruption of our psychic futures would sometimes be a welcome change. As if on psychic cue, Miss Blue would appear with tea and cookies!

The Brabins acquired a television set. It was not appropriate to place a television in the living room so it was placed in the small den off the living room. Most often I would watch television with Uncle Charlie. Theda would prefer to read a book. The programs she liked most included Fireside Theater on CBS and *The Colgate Comedy Hour* on NBC. I remember watching the 1931 version of *Ben-Hur* that Uncle Charlie was involved with directing. As we watched the movie he said, "Pay close attention now and you will see a microphone pop into the picture up in the right hand corner," and then he would laugh. Other directors were involved in making the film; I do not believe Uncle Charlie would have let that happen because he was so meticulous with his work!

I also watched with him, *Sporting Blood* with Clark Gable and *The*

Mask of Fu Manchu starring Boris Karloff. *Sporting Blood* was Clark Gable's first starring role. I was unaware at that time that Uncle Charlie had anything to do with these films. I later learned that he had directed them all!

The photos and memorabilia of the silent films became very familiar to me; however, they represented a past that I could never experi-

Joan Craig, 1955 (photograph Provided by Joan Craig).

ence. I would often look at a photo of Theda and think about all that was involved in taking the picture. It was often a simple pose, but I marveled at how the photo would help create the image of the Vamp, the most iconic image in early film history!

The Last Party

The last party held at the Brabin house was a Southern-style luncheon. It was prepared by our cooks Ann and Hayes Payton. There was lots of fried chicken and a mint julep cake made by Theda. While the food was being transported across the street, Groucho Marx was just walking past with his miniature schnauzer. He wanted a piece of chicken. He said, "I can't get that at home!" Ann lifted the cover, Groucho took a piece, and Ann handed him a napkin!

Some of Theda and Uncle Charlie's friends who came to their home for tea, parties, or small dinner gatherings included Charles Laughton and his wife Elsa Lanchester, Maureen O'Sullivan, Bette Davis, Norma Shearer, Noël Coward, Milton Berle, Imogene Coca, and Ken Murray. Lionel Barrymore came on one occasion. The Brabins attended many gala parties at Pickfair, hosted by Mary Pickford, and at Green Acres, hosted by Mildred and Harold Lloyd.

On June 30, 1954, Theda had an emergency appendectomy with complications. When Theda was well enough, Marion Davies invited her, along with my mother and me, for lunch at Ocean House. Ocean House was a Georgian mansion with 118 rooms, 34 bedrooms, and 55 baths located on the beach front in Santa Monica. It was the most magnificent property. Marion at this time was occupying a small wing of the mansion. The rest of the property was deteriorating.

Marion was very concerned about Theda's health. She wanted to know everything, including her doctor's name. Theda told her that Charlie also needed an operation. As we were departing, Marion put a check in Theda's purse. She said, "You are going to need this. You are my dearest friend and I don't want to lose you. Get the best doctor that you can find."

In August, Uncle Charlie and Theda had operations on the same day, but in different hospitals. When they came home, Miss Blue packed her bags and departed after being there for at least twenty years. They were now alone and both too ill to walk. They would write love notes to each other which I would carry back and forth. Uncle Charlie would always ask me to pick a rose for Theda from the garden.

Ann made meals to take to the Brabins. I would often enter through the back door to the kitchen and sometimes I would find Alfred Hitchcock sitting at the dining room table reading a stack of papers. He would often stop by to see if Theda and Uncle Charlie needed help. Sometimes I would find him in a chair in Uncle Charlie's room trying to cheer him. When I appeared, quietly and without any words he would disappear.

9

My Theda

Be True to Yourself

As soon as Uncle Charlie was able, he became very busy cleaning and polishing the objects of art in the house. I could see there was sadness in his eyes, and that he felt an ending was near. He said to me, "She will be getting better; go to Theda. Just knock and go in. She loves you, you know."

On one of the last days that I saw Theda, I went to her room. She said, "Sit down here with me on the bed. It's all over now. Stay as sweet as you are. When you grow up, be true to yourself; don't try to be anyone else and don't try to be me."

The next day when I arrived, Theda's costumes and jewelry were laid out around her room. She said, "I want you to have them. On the table in the living room is my favorite set of china. It is for you to enjoy and remember me by." Theda had given me some of her most cherished belongings that were part of her life.

Theda quietly passed away on April 7, 1955, at California Lutheran Hospital. On April 10, funeral services were held at Pierce Brothers Mortuary in Beverly Hills for Theda Bara Brabin, the great actress of early silent film, the great Vamp, and my friend, who had loved me unconditionally and had taught me so much about life. I sat with Uncle Charlie and Theda's sister Lori as we listened to the tributes spoken by Rabbi Edgar Magnin. I remember that the words just passed through my head. I realized a part of me was gone and no words could replace my grief and despair. I wasn't even allowed to sign the guest book for fear of the press invading our privacy.

A month later, a tribute for Theda was held at the Church of the Good Shepherd in Beverly Hills. News of the date and time was passed by word of mouth. People in the film industry still feared being blacklisted just by being at the gathering for Theda Bara. The attendants had been notified not to linger or greet anyone on the outside before or after the service. Most of the women who came were heavily veiled and the men tried to bury their faces with their handkerchiefs. Everyone came; the church was filled, leaving standing room only. Uncle Charlie stood at the entrance greeting each person as they came in. He said he never expected such a large turnout. Uncle Charlie, with his broken heart, took my hand and we walked to the front pew. We listened as friends shared their fond memories of Theda.

The Following Years

After Theda's death, Charles Brabin moved to an apartment in Santa Monica near friends. I often visited with him while he was in declining health. He died on November 3, 1957, of heart disease. My mother and I attended to the funeral arrangements for Uncle Charlie at St. Monica's Catholic Church in Santa Monica. Charles Joseph Brabin was interned near Theda at Forest Lawn Memorial Park in Glendale.

Theda's last formal portrait, taken in 1951 for a *Life* magazine article (© John Engstead/mptvimages.com).

Lori Bara continued to live in a small furnished apartment convenient to nearby restaurants in Westwood Village. During her life she often worked as an interpreter. Lori, like Theda, was able to speak fluently in Latin as well as seven other languages. However, she suffered emotionally with the loss of all of her family members. We would meet her for dinner in Westwood so that she would not always dine alone. Lori was interested in preserving her family heritage. She gave me the family documents which included Theda Bara's life story, family photos, and letters belonging to Pauline Louise and Régine de Coppet. The collection contained the letters of Madame de Staël, Lord Byron and the de Broglie family. Many were in a foreign language. Over a period of time Lori declined with Alzheimer's disease and when she needed care we placed her in the care of Marycrest Manor, a Culver City nursing facility founded by Cardinal James Francis McIntyre. (Cardinal McIntyre served as archbishop of Los Angeles from 1948 to 1970.)

In 1961, I traveled to Europe to visit all of the places in Madame de Staël's and Lord Byron's history. By meeting with historians and interpreters, I was able to acquire some additional information regarding Theda's grandmother, Régine de Coppet. These valuable records were placed in a concealed fire safety vault in the home of a friend in Brentwood. On November 6, 1961, Bel-Air and Brentwood became engulfed in a firestorm with 50 MPH winds. The flames burned 495 beautiful homes. When the fire jumped the 405 Freeway we drove directly to my mother's friend's house. We could see the fire raging in the area of the house that contained Theda Bara's family papers.

The fire had moved very quickly and soon we were only allowed to walk up the roads. When we arrived in front of the house there was nothing there, just moldering ash, a green lawn and part of a chimney. Later we sifted

Theda Bara, 1923 (Stout Collection).

through the ashes and nothing of the fire safety vault remained. The irreplaceable documents of Theda Bara and her family were gone.

The most important question has yet to be answered: Was Theda Bara's grandmother the daughter of Madame de Staël and Lord Byron? With the written evidences all burned up, the secret may forever remain with Madame de Staël, or other evidences may yet be found.

Theda Bara gave me her most cherished costumes as a remembrance of her. A few years ago I went alone to an open house Christmas event along a boulevard of antique stores. Many people were enjoying refreshments and holiday cheer when I heard the name Theda Bara in the distance. I followed the sound to a group of people and said, "Did you say Theda Bara?" The young person responded, "Yes, I am a dancer and Theda Bara is my idol but I didn't just speak her name." I responded, "I knew her." She then said, "I know someone who I want you to meet." She introduced me to Hugh Munro Neely and Andi Hicks of Timeline Films who had just produced *The Woman with the Hungry Eyes,* a documentary on the life and times of Theda Bara. I was then introduced to Robert "Bob" Birchard who authored an article in *Statement Magazine* about my childhood with Theda Bara with photographs of Theda's beautiful costumes. I realized that Theda was with me, that she had guided me to the voice that I heard in the distance, which led me to the people that she was so grateful to for preserving her memory and her films.

From that moment on, I realized that my memories of my childhood with Theda Bara were unique. The most precious gift that she gave me is that she shared her life, her friends and all of her life philosophies with me. For that, I will forever be grateful to my friend.

10

The Stage Plays

1908

The Devil

The Devil, written by one of Hungary's most versatile dramatists Ferenc Molnar, opened on Broadway in two different theaters on August 18, 1908. In the play, an adaptation of the Faustian model, a man, Dr. Muller, enjoys tormenting good people for his own pleasure. Muller comes between Marie and her fiancé George in such a manner that George begins to question Marie's devotion to him. Molnar accomplishes this by introducing his character Paul, who becomes the catalyst for this morality tale. George thinks that Paul has taken his fiancé from him; however, it is not true. At the end of the story, Marie prays to the Almighty for strength, and because of her efforts, Dr. Muller goes up in flames. The dramatic story was ideal for theater audiences of that era.

Henry W. Savage and Harrison Grey Fiske, rival theater managers, both claimed that they had the authorized version of *The Devil* and the rights to stage it. Savage issued an announcement that the evening opening at the Garden Theater would be on August 18. He'd originally intended to open on September 28 and claimed that the change was made due to confusion in advertising the opening of Fiske's play. However, it seems likely that Savage's new opening date was set to compete with Fiske's play. Savage also stated that Fiske's play was not authorized by either the author or his agents.

According to a *New York Times* article, both the Belasco and the Garden were filled to capacity on opening day. Fiske's version was staged as a comedy while Savage's version was listed as a tragedy in strict accordance with the production abroad.

Theda (her last name then was de Coppet) made her first stage appearance in the role of Madame Schleswig in Savage's version. While arguments took place regarding the rights to produce the play, it was the only time in the history of the theater that audiences could view two entirely different adaptations of the same play produced by two different people opening on the same day. Theda was offered the role of Madame Schleswig by Fiske; however, she accepted Savage's offer. She considered the unusual events to be a fateful omen.

Theda kept both of the original play books as keepsakes. When she brought them out for me to read, she also brought out two masks. She laid them on the table next to the play books, explaining that one mask was the theatrical symbol for comedy and the other the theatrical symbol for tragedy.

1912

The Quaker Girl

Theda Bara, c. 1919 (Stout Collection).

In the fall of 1912, Theda became part of the road tour of the musical comedy *The Quaker Girl*. Its limited run took Theda west to Los Angeles, Portland and the state of Washington. The company was headed by Victor Morley and it starred DeWolf Hopper. DeWolf's wife, Hedda Hopper (later the famous gossip columnist), played the role of Mathilde. Hopper noted in her book *From Under My Hat* that Theda Bara "played a French woman with an accent that wouldn't fool a five-year-old." Hopper didn't realize that Theda's accent and dialect was Francoprovençal; however, she certainly realized it wasn't Parisian French! Theda disliked traveling in the road tour. The accommodations were poor and she had to share a room. She later said that it was a terrible experience.

1920

The Blue Flame

Theda's career in silent films took precedence over the theater. She did not return to the stage until 1920 when she played the role of Ruth Gordon in *The Blue Flame*. When Theda read the script she envisioned lavish costumes, sensational stage effects and wicked scenes. She was convinced that *The Blue Flame* would be the perfect play for her because of its unusual storyline: A young girl killed by lightning returns to life as a vampire without a soul. It was familiar territory; not quite the Vamp, but something akin to it. The melodrama opened in Boston with Theda, who by then was internationally known as "The Vamp." The play attracted rioting playgoers who wanted to see Theda in person. After playing to great crowds in several cities, *The Blue Flame* was scheduled to open at the Schubert Theater on Broadway.

However, on March 13, 1920, the *New York Times* reported: "Owen Davis, a well known author, claims rights to *The Blue Flame*." In response, A.W. Woods, the producer, said that the play was adapted from a story by Leta Nicholson Vance. The script was written by George V. Hobart and John Willard. Woods had purchased the play for $35,000. The article went on to state: "Owen Davis declares that he will have his attorneys file an injunction the day after *The Blue Flame* opens to halt the play. He is claiming that *The Blue Flame* is founded on his novel, *Lola*."

The Schubert Theater was packed on opening night with critics and such celebrities as Mae Murray, Norma Talmadge, Geraldine Farrar, Florence Reed, and Lewis Selznick. Many of Theda's film fans were in attendance. Owen Davis and Leta Nicholson Vance were also in the audience.

After Davis watched the performance he stated, "I certainly never wrote this!" Vance sent a letter to the *New York Times* stating that she was in attendance on opening night and that she found the play "strange, very strange." She also stated that she could not recognize a line in the play as being in the original manuscript. She was extremely upset with the adaptation, stating, "This drama now being played does not bear resemblance to any work of mine. Please publish my disavowal of authorship."

Questions arose about the play. Was it a comedy or was it a tragedy? It was stated by some that the script was so lacking that it was funny. Despite the confusion surrounding the play, the newspapers noted that there were larger numbers of fans at the stage door than ever before in its history. Audiences continued to swarm to see Theda, despite the fact that it was labeled by many critics as a bad play. One particularly harsh reviewer, Heywood Broun, noted, "[Bara] made a speech in which she said that God had been very kind to her. Probably she referred to the fact that at no time during the course of the evening did the earth open and swallow up the authors, the star, and all the company."

Theda stated, "On opening night at the Schubert Theater, everything possible went wrong. Actors skipped lines and entered onto the

Theda in the play *The Blue Flame*, c. 1920 (Stout Collection).

stage at the wrong time. When I fell onto the couch my skirt rose above my knees and I couldn't pull my skirt down as I was supposed to be dead! The machine that was supposed to resurrect me from the dead failed to work."

Theda's response to the public was, "To be good is to be forgotten. I'm going to be so bad I'll be remembered always." After forty-eight performances at the Schubert Theater, *The Blue Flame* went on tour for a year and prospered. Fortunately for Theda, she owned fifty percent of it.

11

The Films

1914

The Stain

Theda's film career began when she heard about the filming of *The Stain* at Pathé Films. Frank Powell had selected her to work as an extra in a scene with Virginia Pearson and Edward José. It was filmed in the garden of a monastery. When Powell viewed the scene, he noticed that Theda was much more the femme fatale than Pearson ever could be. Theda's role was so well acted that the scene couldn't be used and wound up on the cutting floor. Theda, who did not mince words, said that she made Virginia Pearson look bad and that she was more suitable for the lead role. (Theda's assessment of her talent was correct. She had also learned that timidity would not get her very far in such a competitive industry.) When she heard that the scene had been cut, she asked Powell why he had done so. It is not known what Powell's explanation was, but he surely must have provided an answer that placated Theda. He did tell her that he could use another nun in a scene to be filmed later that day. Theda immediately went to the wardrobe room and found that there were only two nun habits. She rushed home, made her costume, and returned in time for the filming. Theda is recognizable by her habit collar because it is a little different from the others.

1915

A Fool There Was

Robert Hilliard's *A Fool There Was*, starring Virginia Pearson, played on Broadway in 1909 at New York's Liberty Theater. It was an

11. The Films

adaptation of Rudyard Kipling's *The Vampire*. William Fox purchased the screen rights and hired Frank Powell to direct it. Powell remembered Theda's exotic beauty on screen and her ability to make dramatic facial expressions. Powell immediately placed her in the starring role of the vampire, and with that casting, Theda's movie career was launched and there would be no turning back. She became a megastar when *A Fool There Was* began playing. Audiences couldn't get enough of her.

Theda had decided that in order to create a mysterious, larger-than-life persona, she would change her name. After much thought, she decided on Theda Bara; the first name originated from her childhood nickname, Teddy, and the last name was derived from her grandfather's surname, Baranger. Theda explained to Fox press agents Al Selig and Johnny Goldfrap that Bara spelled backwards was Arab. Selig and Goldfrap liked the name and, being the good press agents they were, they immediately claimed that the name was an anagram for Arab Death. This mysterious observation was exactly the fuel that Selig and Goldfrap needed to create the persona of the beautiful woman who audiences saw on the big screen. To add to the hype, they publicized Theda Bara as "The vampire, the wickedest woman in the world!"

Prior to the opening of *A Fool There Was*, Theda was informed by her publicists that she must hold press conferences in her hotel rooms. Theda, eager to build

Theda Bara, c. 1920 (Stout Collection).

her career, decorated the rooms with Egyptian statues, tiger skins, and symbols of the occult. The air was full of incense. The press was told that she was accustomed to the desert climate of her native Egypt. Once when they arrived, they found Theda, reclining on a chaise lounge, draped in a velvet cloak in an overheated hotel room. She dramatically announced to the assembled reporters, "I was raised in a huge tent not far from the Sphinx. This oasis was our little home for years and was to us like the Garden of Eden. My mother taught me the languages, expression, and the art of pantomime. My father taught me how to paint and how to see the beauty and combination of colors. Through the instruction of both, I learned the symphony of the soul."

Newspaper reporters dutifully reported that Theda Bara was born "in the shadows of the pyramids, the only daughter of a French actress who saved the life of an Italian artist lost in a desert of Egyptian sands." They also reported that she was "the wickedest woman in the world," "Satan's handmaiden," and "The Devil's Daughter." Theda, with her long black hair, blood red lips, intense, penetrating kohl-rimmed eyes, corpse-pale skin, curvy buxom figure, and scandalous skin-revealing gowns, brought a new kind of femme fatale to the screen. "The Vamp" was described as "a sexual vampire who sapped and drained men's vital energies to the dregs, and left them more dead than alive." There was always a trail of death and destruction in her wake, "broken men with lost and shattered souls." The exotically beautiful Vamp would do nothing to ease their suffering; a scornful laugh was all that was offered. Then "the devourer of men's souls," giddy with her power, went mercilessly on to her next victim.

Louella Parsons, a syndicated columnist, wrote in the *St. Petersburg Times* on November 8, 1947: "One of the most hilarious interviews was with Theda Bara in Chicago. It was in the days when she was pretending to be born in the shadow of the Sphinx. Although the day was hotter than the proverbial hinges, she was swathed to the teeth in furs, because she [supposedly] couldn't get used to our northern weather. "

A Fool There Was, directed by Frank Powell from a screenplay by Powell and Roy L. McCardell, was released in January 1915. As a prelude to the film's showing, Rudyard Kipling's poem "The Vampire" was read. Portions of the poem were used as intertitles in the film.

In *A Fool There Was,* Theda plays the Vampire, a woman who sets her sights on John Schuyler, a married lawyer who is sent overseas to work as a diplomat for the U.S. government in England. Schuyler falls

11. The Films

Theda Bara in *A Fool There Was* (1915) (Stout Collection).

for the beautiful vampire after simply catching a glimpse of her ankle on the passenger ship. From that one moment his fate is sealed. The Vampire uses him mercilessly to the point of destroying his soul. In the final scene, the Vampire is seen smiling as she drops rose petals on Schuyler's dying body. Theda's fame was assured when "The Vamp" was born.

One scene, filmed on the beach at St. Augustine, Florida, showed Theda wearing a bathing suit. Censors removed it because it was too risqué for a woman to appear in a bathing suit on film at that time. Despite its deletion, *A Fool There Was* went on to become such a box office smash that Fox was able to establish Fox Studios in Fort Lee, New Jersey, as a major motion picture company. Theda Bara became the first overnight instant celebrity and the first femme fatale of the silver screen.

Hundreds of thousands of fans around the world wanted to see her. By the end of 1915, Theda had starring roles in ten films. The vampire films had become a sensation. Women appeared in vampire-styled gowns; pendant earrings became hot. They also began to apply more colorful makeup, instead of the white opaque look of the past. It became the rage to accentuate the eyes with color; red was now a desirable color for the lips.

A Fool There Was was the first film banned by Britain's official censor. Although Theda was drawing large audiences and was sensationalized in the newspapers, she became the target of morals groups who were calling for the banning of her films.

1915

The Kreutzer Sonata

Theda's next film, *The Kreutzer Sonata*, directed by Herbert Brenon, was released on March 18, 1915. She was now recognized as "the greatest emotional actress." The original play, adapted from the works of Leo Tolstoy, was written by a Russian, Jacob Gordin. The original story, published in 1889, was promptly censored by Russian authorities. The United States prohibited the mailing of newspapers containing serialized portions of the story.

Featuring the required twists and turns of movies of that era, it told of a child born out of wedlock, jealousy, an illicit love affair, confrontation, and payback. While there was visually nothing offensive in the film, it could not be shown to any person under the age of 21.

The Clemenceau Case

The Clemenceau Case, Theda's third film, released in April 1915, was also directed by Herbert Brenon. On July 4, 1915, the *Pittsburgh Press* reported: "Theda Bara has never been seen to better advantage than in the picture play based on Alexandre Dumas' novel, *The Clemenceau Case*. [It's] a film drama peculiarly suited to the display of Miss Bara's great genius at its best. The character of Iza, the beautiful woman with the basilisk soul, whose diversion is luring men on to love and ruin, affords her an opportunity to give a rendition of this most remarkable part that will scorch the memories of her spectators like a living flame."

11. The Films

Theda's Iza is a beautiful, sensual girl of fifteen who commits immoral acts and lacks gratitude. Theda considered the role to be most interesting. It was one of her favorite roles, one that allowed her to present the psychological aspects of a siren. She wears a black laced scarf wrapped three times around her head with only her eyes showing as she tells her pursuers that no other man has looked upon her.

Theda as Iza in *The Clemenceau Case*, 1915 (Stout Collection).

In the film, Theda used a stuffed snake as a prop. She kept it her entire life. Theda also cherished a small book with her face on the cover, an edition of *The Clemenceau Case* that was printed at the time of the film. The book was also used as a prop in the picture.

The Devil's Daughter

Released shortly after *The Clemenceau Case* on June 16, 1915, *The Devil's Daughter* was directed by Frank Powell and based on *La Gioconda* by Gabriele D'Annunzio. As La Gioconda, Theda is the embodiment of an evil but beautiful siren who is half serpent and half woman by nature. She uses pantomime to convey the deadly warning of a scorned and cast-aside woman: "As this man has done to me so shall I do to all men. From now on my heart is ice, my passion consuming fire. Let men beware!"

Theda kept the costume she wore as La Gioconda. Years later she showed it to me. From the waist down to the feet, it was in the form of a fish.

Theda as La Gioconda with an unidentified actor in *The Devil's Daughter*, 1915 (Stout Collection).

Lady Audley's Secret

Lady Audley's Secret, starring Theda as the "The Satanic Sorceress of the Screen," was released on August 8, 1915. It was directed by Marshall Farnum. It was a remake of a film made in 1912 with Herbert Brenon as director and Jane Fearnley as Lady Audley.

The story has its share of unique twists and turns. Lady Audley, a woman with a past and *more* than one secret, shoves her lover down a well. When he reappears, she goes insane. Madness, bigamy, attempted murder, and seduction combine to make a film which audiences couldn't resist. It was said that not another artist could have portrayed the part of the mad Lady Audley with such thrilling power as did Theda Bara!

The Two Orphans

The Two Orphans opened on September 5, 1915. Herbert Brenon not only directed this film but he also appeared in the role of Pierre, a

Theda as Henriette with William E. Shay as Chevalier de Vaudrey in *The Two Orphans*, 1915 (Stout Collection).

cripple. The Fox production was based on a play called *Two Orphans*, successful in the late 1800s. The story was about an orphan who takes care of her blind sister in Paris. William Fox felt strongly that the play would be destined for success on the big screen and he spent $200,000 to produce it. The tabloids which sensationalized the vampire films brought crowds of people to the new and elaborate movie theaters. However, the publicists declined to promote Theda in a heroic role and disregarded the critics' praise of her performance. This role was said to be one of Theda's favorites.

Sin

Theda Bara as Rosa in *Sin*, 1915. On April 27, 1994, a 29-cent stamp was released by the United States Postal service depicting Theda Bara with a likeness to the *Sin* photograph (lower right corner of the photograph). It was part of their commemorative issue of stamps honoring silent screen stars. The stamp was designed from a drawing by Al Hirschfeld (Stout Collection).

On October 3, 1915, William Fox presented this "Photoplay Supreme" to the moviegoing public. This time Fox dispensed with all niceties to ensure large vampire-seeking crowds. To do that, he simply entitled the film *Sin*. Also known as "the earliest version of *Dr. Jekyll and Mr. Hyde*," it was written and directed by Herbert Brenon. Theda, billed as "the world's wickedest woman" and with her hair like the serpent locks of Medusa, played Rosa. She wears jewels to a mobster meeting where Warner Oland, as Pietro, denounces her as being sacrilegious. Rosa is torn to shreds by an angry religious throng while Luigi kills himself before an altar over his guilt in the theft of the jewels. The photoplay was a box office success. It was banned in Theda's home state of Ohio as well as Georgia.

Carmen

In 1915, the Metropolitan Opera House in New York City was packed with people wanting to see the all-star stage production *Carmen*, starring Geraldine Farrar, Enrico Caruso and the Italian conductor Arturo Toscanini. The house was filled to capacity each night while the box office was forced to turn away others still standing in lines to get in. Gossip was abundant at that time about Geraldine Farrar having an affair with Toscanini, a married man with children. He eventually chose to resign after nearly five hundred performances and returned to Italy.

William Fox quickly decided to purchase the rights to the opera in order to bring it to the screen. Fox's version would be based on the opera as written by Georges Bizet. The company had elaborate sets built at Fort Lee and hired the talented Raoul Walsh to write the screenplay and direct. Edward Velasquez was brought from Seville to supervise the technical and architectural details of the Spanish sets created in the Fox studios. Spanish palaces, plazas, cathedrals and stores were recreated. An Andalusian bull was imported from Madrid to lunge and charge in a replica of the bullring of Seville. The Azure Baths of Cordova is where Don Jose (played by Elmer Linden, known as the world's greatest mime) first encounters the flirtatious Theda Bara as Carmen.

It has been said that Walsh produced the film without a technical or artistic flaw. During one rehearsal, a famous admirer appeared on set and left a gift for Theda. When she opened the box, inside was a large, beautifully crafted dagger with a card signed Pancho Villa, the renowned Mexican Revolutionary general!

Theda as Carmen, from the movie *Carmen*, 1915 (Stout Collection).

Theda's *Carmen* was not the only film version. In 1913, Jesse Lasky, Samuel Goldwyn and Cecil B. DeMille formed the Jesse L. Lasky Feature Play Company located in Hollywood and in their 1915 *Carmen*, DeMille cast Geraldine Ferrar as Carmen and Wallace Reid as Don Jose. Lasky's *Carmen* was based on the novel by Prosper Merimee and directed by DeMille. While filming at the Lasky Studios, Geraldine met and fell in love with Lou Tellegen, the handsome matinee idol of the stage and leading man to Sarah Bernhardt. Tellegen and Farrar married in February 1916.

Being of a competitive nature, the Lasky Company released their *Carmen* on the same day as the Fox version. Both were successful. Some critics described Lasky's *Carmen* as "remarkable." One wrote, "Farrar's acting is able and bold." Another critic wrote of Theda's *Carmen*, "[Miss Bara] displays her excellent character portrayal as the beautiful Spanish gypsy. She appears seductive without objectionable elements."

Theda's *Carmen* was passed by the censors; Farrar's *Carmen* was not. In Philadelphia, the Pennsylvania Board of Motion Picture Censors

Theda as Francesca Brabaut and Stuart Holmes as Antoine Brabaut in *The Galley Slave*, 1915 (Stout Collection).

declared Farrar's acting in certain portions of the Lasky picture to be shocking and improper. Some footage was ordered removed. Movie houses across the nation continued to open both versions on the same day, providing audiences the opportunity to view and compare both.

The Galley Slave

Within a month of the release of *Carmen*, Fox Studios released its next film *The Galley Slave* on November 28, 1915. Theda was billed as "The Archangel of Destiny" as Francesca Brabaut. Stuart Holmes played Francesca's evil husband while Claire Whitney had the role of Cecil Blaine. Bartley Campbell's celebrated drama tells the story of an artist's model and the poor painter who weds her. He leaves her when he comes into some money.

Destruction

Determined to get the most out of his main star, William Fox managed to release one more Bara film that year. Theda must have been worn nearly to a frazzle by the time *Destruction* was released on December 26, 1915. However, youth was still on her side: She was only 30 years old in 1915.

Destruction was directed by Will S. Davis, who also wrote the screenplay (adapted from French author Emile Zola's novel *Destruction*). Theda is Fernande, an evil woman who plunges thousands of working men's families into poverty and suffering. The film exposed the evil of underpayment to laborers.

1916

The Serpent

The Serpent, released January 23, 1916, was directed by Raoul Walsh. An adaptation of Phillip Bartholomae's *The Wolf's Claw*, it was written by Walsh's younger brother George. Theda plays Vania, a Rus-

Theda Bara with J. Gordon Edwards, director (right), and his son Jack Edwards (left), home from Cornell University (Stout Collection).

sian peasant girl who seeks revenge on the lecherous grand duke who murdered her lover. The film features realistic scenes of Russian life. One intense scene takes the audience on a real wild boar hunt. The battles were also visually real and portrayed the struggles between the Teutonic Allies and the Russians. These scenes were filmed on location at Chimney Rock near Asheville, North Carolina.

Because Theda had proved to be a cash cow for Fox, he spared no expense on her films. For *Destruction*, Raoul Walsh hired military experts to supervise the maneuvers. For one scene, a large area of ground was dug out with the intent to capture on film a real explosion occurring just after soldiers passed over a mine. But the wrong signal was given to the man operating the electrical connection and he closed the switch too soon. The premature explosion injured many of the players. Guns and swords flew high into the air.

At theaters in various cities, groups of protestors stated that the film was immoral. Theda responded by saying, "I have just as definite a place, just as high a mission in pictures as the best of your evangelists and the most beloved of your ministers."

Gold and the Woman

Gold and the Woman, released on March 15, 1916, and directed by James Vincent, tells the story of an Indian's curse and the Mexican Revolution. Theda plays Juliet Cordova, a Mexican aristocrat's daughter who longs for wealth. As the movie progresses, an entire Indian camp is blown up. When Juliet's father's house is attacked by revolutionists, she dresses in a suit of armor and marches out from the burning building, leaving the bandits gaping at the strange appearance.

Theda as Vania Lazar in *The Serpent*, 1916 (Stout Collection).

The film broke movie house records. On March 16, 1916, the *Pittsburgh Press* stated, "The picture that was advertised a week ago but delayed by the censors at Harrisburg, *Gold and the Woman*, is to be presented. As usual Theda Bara scores a triumph in the part she portrays."

Theda believed that her body was beautiful and that plumpness was an attraction. She had an aversion to corsets and believed that wearing one was unhealthy. She designed and created most all of her film wardrobes. Her mother created the hairpieces and wigs. Theda was an incredible artist who envisioned not only the role but created the image.

Audiences packed the movie houses to see Theda Bara. Many

Harry Hilliard as Lee Duskara and Theda as Juliet Cordova in *Gold and the Woman*, 1916 (Stout Collection).

believed that she was not only a vamp on screen, but a vamp in her real life as well. Those views held by many became a dual-edged sword for Theda.

THEDA TALKS TO THE PUBLIC

On April 10, 1916, the *Pittsburgh Press* printed an article by Theda Bara written especially for the press. In it, she asks:

> Would you like to be called a love pirate, an Ishmaelite of femininity, a vampire, or the woman with the most beautiful wicked face in the world? That is what people call me because of the parts I play in the Fox Film Corporation's production of *Carmen, A Fool There Was, The Clemenceau Case, Sin,* and *The Devil's Daughter*. Pretty nearly everyone in the country has told what he or she thinks of me and now for the first time I am given an opportunity to tell what I think of myself! Vampiring such as I do, is the hardest kind of hard

work. I am imbued with the character and lose myself in it. Complete exhaustion follows my day of work. A year ago, when my name was displayed on the billboards for the first time, the American people did not know whether it was a new toothpaste, soap, or a malady. Now when they see it, they invariably say, "the human vampire."

It is not pleasant to be so described. When I first heard myself referred to as "the vampire woman," I was heartbroken. All my ideals were shattered. I felt I was that against which every woman's hand is raised. I was held up as one who delighted in the lure of destruction and evil-doing. People asked what manner of woman I could be. One woman wrote this description of me:

Sheet music entitled "Theda Bara (I'll Keep Away From You) (Stout Collection).

"Her hair is like the serpent locks of Medusa, her eyes have the cruel cunning of Lucrezia Borgia, till now held up as the wickedest woman of the world. Her mouth is the mouth of the sinister, scheming Delilah, and her hands are those of the blood-bathing Elizabeth Bathory, who slaughtered young girls that she might bathe in their warm life blood and so retain her beauty. Can it be that fate has reincarnated in Theda Bara the souls of these monsters of medieval times?"

Hardly a day passes that the postman does not bring me letters written along similar lines. Many of them attack me most unmercifully. Some intimate that no woman could portray such characters without actual experience. Here is a type of letter I received during the past few months:

"You are a menace to the human race. Man is a mere toy in your hands or those of women like you. Your type inevitably leads to ruin and destruction. Those glittering eyes of yours are like those of the serpent, except that they are more dangerous!"

Such letters hurt. It is impossible to accustom myself to them. Who do people hate me so? I try to show the world how attractive sin may be, how very beautiful so that one must be always on the lookout and know evil even in disguise. I am a moral teacher then, if many people go to see me and receive my message as I mean to give it to them. But what is my reward? I am detested. People seem to forget that I am only an actress; that an actress should never show her real self to an audience else she ceases to be an actress.

A woman in New York saw my photograph in a frame in front of a theater and deliberately jabbed a hole through my face with her umbrella. But why do people hate me so?

While some of my best parts show me as a soulless creature, I think they are susceptible to defense and I believe the "vampire woman" can be justified as a type. I think there is a great moral lesson taught in most of the plays in which I have appeared.

The Milwaukee Sentinel stated on May 26, 1916: "Mayor Puchta of Cincinnati listened seriously to recent protests from certain sources against the exhibition of photoplays in which Theda Bara appeared in that city. Miss Bara came to her defense with a letter in which she said in part:

> I cannot conceive why my appearance in pictures in Cincinnati theaters could give ground or cause for the protests that are now being published in dispatches from Cincinnati. I cannot analyze or understand the purpose of those who would seek to attach stigma to my name because of the work I have done in pictures which have been exhibited in your city. Quite to the contrary, every mother, minister, every person with the well being of the younger elements of the city owes me some gratitude for what I have accomplished through these pictures. Every picture in which I have appeared has a clear and understandable moral. The ministers of your city have a definite aim and purpose in their work and achieve much. To pillory me for trying earnestly, through my pictures, to make sin and wrongdoing a thing to be shunned and avoided presents an inconsistency which I am unable to fathom. I have just as definite a place, just as high a mission in pictures as the best of your evan-

Theda reads fan mail (Stout Collection).

gelists and the most beloved of your local ministers. Through the silent but expressive medium of the motion picture I am saving hundreds of girls from social degradation.

The Eternal Sapho

At Theda's request, Bertram Bracken was hired to direct *The Eternal Sapho*. It was released on May 7, 1916. Mary Murillo's screenplay is based upon French author Alphonse Daudet's novel *Sapho*. Fox hired Rial Schellinger as cinematographer to capture Theda as Laura Bruffin in a powerfully intense love story. Laura is rescued from the fury of a drunken father and brought to the Paris studio of an artist named Coudal. He is

Theda as Laura Bruffins in *The Eternal Sapho*, 1916 (Stout Collection).

soon infatuated and Laura becomes his model. Laura, an unscrupulous and unprincipled woman, is attracted to other men, so a tragic ending is inevitable. Theda's portrayal of Laura was so terribly tragic that experts in the field of film stated that the picture was Bara's masterpiece. Also noted was the fact that Theda wore very unusual costumes.

East Lynne

Mary Braddon, author of thrillers and novels of psychological mystery, wrote the stage adaptation of Mrs. Henry Wood's novel *East Lynne*. The five-reel feature utilizes a modernized American scenario crafted by Mary Murillo. Directed by Bertram Bracken, *East Lynne* was released on June 19, 1916.

Theda plays the beautiful villainess Lady Isabel Carlisle. The film opens with the sale of an estate, East Lynne, to satisfy the creditors of John Severn. Young barrister Archibald Carlisle (Ben Deeley) falls in love and marries Severn's daughter Lady Isabel. Misrepresentations of others and crimes committed cause Carlisle to divorce Lady Isabel. She subsequently is involved in a train wreck and Carlisle thinks that she is dead. Carlisle then marries Barbara. Lady Isabel disguises herself and

11. The Films 133

becomes the governess of her own children. When her son becomes critically ill, in agony of grief she discloses her identity to her son. At that moment, Carlisle enters the room and recognizes Isabel.

The supporting cast included Stuart Holmes, Claire Whitney, William H. Tooker, Eugenie Woodward, Stanhope Wheatcroft and the Steuart children, Loel and Eldean.

Theda was in a terrifying accident while filming *East Lynne*. She had just completed filming a train wreck scene. She and assistant director Robert Ross were returning to New York City from Fox Studios when her car, driven by her chauffeur, skidded and spun around in pouring rain, landing against a truck hauling iron pipe. During those moments, Theda thought that this was the end of her life. She was hurled to the floor of the car and Ross and the chauffeur received cuts from the broken glass. Because of the accident, Theda never wanted to learn to drive and was always nervous riding in cars.

Stuart Holmes as Captain Levison and Theda as Lady Isabel Carlisle in *East Lynne*, 1916 (Stout Collection).

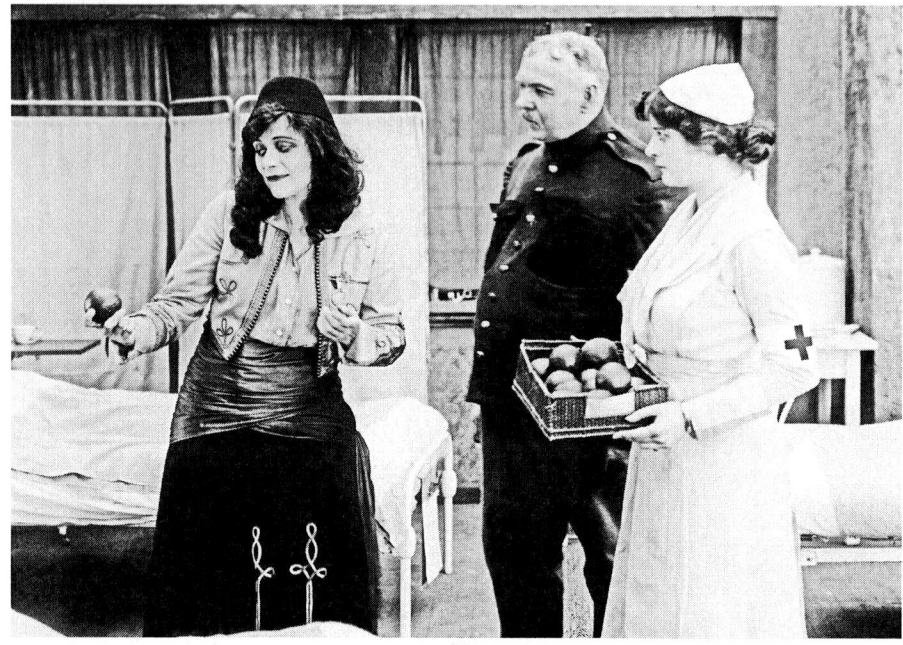

Theda as Cigarette in *Under Two Flags*, 1916, with Maclyn Arbuckle as a soldier and Blanch Bates as a nurse (Stout Collection).

Under Two Flags

Herbert Heyes was cast as Theda's romantic lead in Ouida's novel, *Under Two Flags*, released on July 30, 1916. Director J. Gordon Edwards captured the Algerian desert atmosphere in a story that depicts a regiment of soldiers from different countries. Theda plays Cigarette, a young and adorable tomboy who carries water for the regiment. Because she is good at her job, she eventually works her way up into a heroic, adventurous soldier girl. Bertie Cecil, a soldier serving under the French flag, is forced to make a choice between two flags, the flag of England and the flag of France, when he falls in love with Cigarette. Cigarette dies in the arms of Bertie, sacrificing her life for the cause.

Her Double Life

Theda was finally granted a reprieve from the vamp role with the selection of *Her Double Life* as Fox's next film. J. Gordon Edwards

Stuart Holmes as Lloyd Stanley and Theda as Mary Doone in *Her Double Life*, 1916 (Stout Collection).

directed the film which was released on September 10, 1916. It is the story of Mary Doone, a woman who rises from life in the London slums by taking the place of someone whom she believes to be dead. Doone attains one of the highest ranks in English society, but falls suddenly when the deception is disclosed.

Romeo and Juliet

Two different presentations of *Romeo and Juliet* opened within several days of each other in recognition of the 300th anniversary of Shakespeare's death. In 1916, Metro Pictures began production of their film version starring "the handsomest man in the world," Francis X. Bushman, as Romeo. At the same time, Fox Studios was also secretly in production of *Romeo and Juliet* with "the most famous vamp in the world," Theda Bara as Juliet.

Fox's version is a 70-minute film with 413 scenes shot in 68 different places. It required the studio to replicate a 14th century Verona and a large country estate. The Fox film featured 21 characters, 127 minor performers, and about 2,500 supernumeraries as stated in *The Nevada Daily Mail* on March 15, 1917. An article in *The Day Newspaper* on December 21, 1916, stated, "The film version was as near the text of the play as possible. An entire legion of artists at Fox Studios was employed in fashioning scenery, arranging details, and providing background for the classic story."

On December 31, 1916, it was reported in the *Pittsburgh Press* that the Fox *Romeo and Juliet* "is considered one of the finest films in which Theda Bara has appeared. The atmosphere is as Shakespeare intended and is carried out with an air of realism that grips the attention of the audience." Another news outlet stated, "Theda Bara doesn't act her part, she lives it!"

Alice Gale as the nurse and Theda as Juliet, from the film *Romeo and Juliet*, 1916 (Stout Collection).

Metro's *Romeo and Juliet* spared no expense in replicating the streets of Verona. Those scenes were filmed in Brighton Beach, Brooklyn. Critics reviewing both films stated that Fox's version had better interiors while Metro's version had more elaborate exterior scenes. Audiences had the opportunity to see and compare the films because they ran in theaters at the same time.

The Vixen

The Vixen, a remake of *The Kreutzer Sonata*, opened on December 3, 1916, with Herbert Heyes as Theda's co-star. Under the direction of J. Gordon Edwards, Theda returns to the vampire role of Elsie Drummond, a young society girl. The story tells of the despair felt by a woman

Theda as Elsie Drummond in *The Vixen*, 1916 (Stout Collection).

Theda as Esmeralda in *The Darling of Paris*, 1917 (Stout Collection).

who cannot appreciate or understand the meaning of love. Elsie lures several lovers away from her sister. She gets rid of the one that loses his money and keeps the one who retains his money.

1917

The Darling of Paris

When it was released on January 22, 1917, *The Darling of Paris* was advertised as appearing in "Super Deluxe Screen Format." It was the film version of French author Victor Hugo's immortal romantic tragedy *The Hunchback of Notre Dame*. The studio spared no expense recreating the Cathedral of Notre Dame. The cast included Glen White as the hunchback, Walter Law as Claude Frollo, and Herbert Heyes as Captain Phoebus. Thousands of people were used in the various scenes.

11. The Films

According to one report, "Theda, as the gypsy girl dancer Esmeralda, is to be the best that she has been seen in. Esmeralda, sweet and winsome, obtains the entire sympathy of the audience in her tragic adventures."

Theda Bara (with fur), Lori Bara (center) and William Fox (black bowler hat) sell war bonds in front of the New York Public Library (Stout Collection).

The Tiger Woman

The Tiger Woman, directed by George Bellamy and J. Gordon Edwards, was released on February 18, 1917. This was the second "Super Deluxe" seven-part production produced by Fox Studios.

Princess Petrovitch (Theda) is a woman devoid of a soul, a hard, cruel siren. Bribe money is exchanged between a Russian prince and a Japanese spy. The princess catches them in the act and reports the prince to the Russian secret police. The prince is arrested and the princess leaves for her lover, Count Zorstorf in Monte Carlo. In an intense scene at the Monte Carlo Casino, the count loses all of his money. The princess, cold as the North Sea, poisons the count and flees. On board a ship to America she meets the son of a millionaire. He becomes a murderer to satisfy the princess' desire for money and jewels. The photoplay ends when Princess Petrovitch is forced

Theda as Princess Petrovitch and Emil De Varney as The Count in *The Tiger Woman*, 1917 (Stout Collection).

against her will by a blackmailing servant to plunge a dagger into her own heart.

The supporting cast included Glen White, Mary Martin, and Herbert Heyes. Theda wears numerous beautiful gowns throughout the film.

Her Greatest Love

Her Greatest Love, adapted by Adrian Johnson from Ouida's novel *Moths*, was released on April 2, 1917. Theda plays Hazel, an innocent girl forced by her mother's ambition to marry the cruel Russian Prince Zouroff (Walter Law). Glen White plays Lord Jura and Harry Hilliard portrays Lucies Coresze. The film was considered a box office disaster. Reviewers were very critical of Theda's work, many considering it her worst performance.

Heart and Soul

On May 21, 1917, *Heart and Soul* was released. The story was adapted by Adrian Johnson from *Jess* by famed author H. Rider Haggard. Under the direction of J. Gordon Edwards, *Heart and Soul* was filmed in St. Augustine, Florida. Theda was welcomed back by the locals who remembered her previous film, *A Fool There Was* (1915).

Jess (Theda), the heroine, rides a horse at the head of a regiment of United States troops. She is shot and falls from her mount as the horse continues at a furious pace. Jess soon travels with her mother and sister toward the Hawaiian sugar plantation of her uncle but her mother dies en route. Jess promises that she will always look after her younger sister. She makes the ultimate sacrifice so that her sister may marry John Neil, the man they both love. The supporting actors were Walter Law, Claire Whitney, Harry Hilliard, and Glen White. Again the critics were not kind to Theda. It can be argued that Theda had been worked to exhaustion by Fox. Too many releases in too short a time must have taken its toll on the star. Spectators who watched the filming were amazed at Theda's horsemanship.

Camille

Camille was produced by J. Gordon Edwards and adapted for film by Adrian Johnson from the Alexandre Dumas novel *La Dame aux Camelias* (known simply as *Camille* in the English editions). Dumas' main character was inspired by his love for the courtesan and salon hostess Marie Duplessis, a very pretty and intelligent woman of the time. Marie became Dumas' mistress but the love of her life was Franz Liszt. The original novel, being censored upon its release, was made available to the public by Napoleon Bonaparte. This 1850s popular novel became the basis for Verdi's opera, *La Traviata*.

Vicious and beautiful, Camille is a celebrated courtesan of the French underworld with a string of wealthy lovers. When she falls in love with young Armand Duval, Duval's father feels that Camille will ruin his son's hopes for a secure future and he asks Camille not to marry Armand. Camille relents and leaves Armand. When she falls on hard times and becomes terminally ill, she finds that Armand still loves her. She dies a tragic death.

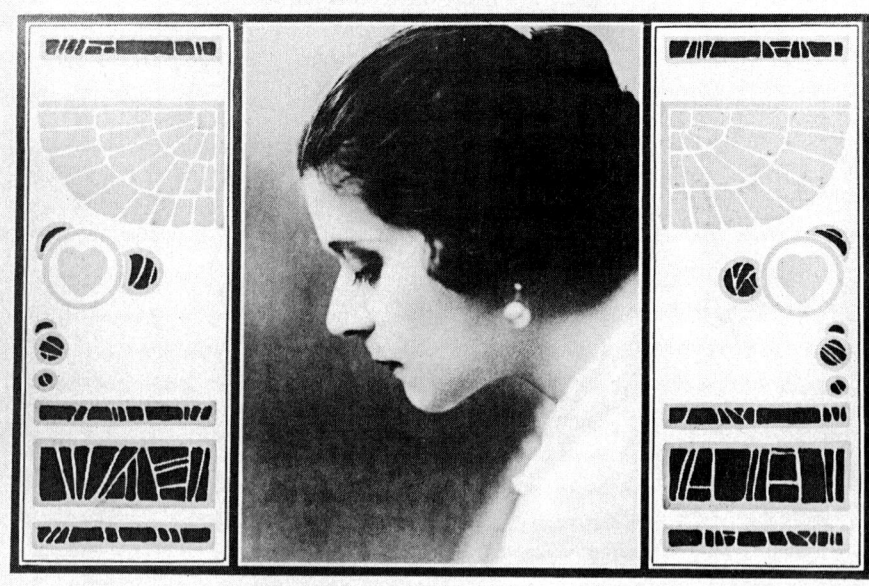

Theda as Jess in *Heart and Soul*, 1917 (Stout Collection).

Theda as Jess in *Heart and Soul*, 1917 (Stout Collection).

Theda as Camille is vivid with a bigger-than-life personality; she is a lover of life. Her leading man, the tall and handsome Albert Roscoe, played the role of Armand beautifully. Supporting actors included Walter Law and Glen White, who had appeared in many of Theda's previous films.

Cleopatra

Theda Bara, the "Serpent of the Nile," attended the grand opening of J. Gordon Edwards' production of *Cleopatra* at the Lyric Theater in New York City on October 14, 1917. Playing the siren of the ages, the Cleopatra of all Cleopatras, she appeared with Fritz Leiber as Caesar and Thurston Hall as Antony. The screenplay was written by Adrian Johnson and Theda. Theda wrote the scenes portraying the marriage of Antony and Cleopatra and also her death scene. She wears a crown with a vulture headpiece that she designed. The piece was made with silk threads in a pattern and color to resemble feathers. Theda was paid

Alice Gale as Madame Prudence with Theda as Marguerite Gautier in *Camille*, 1917 (Stout Collection).

by Fox for authorship with the jewels that she had designed as part of her costumes.

The program for the film's opening declares, "Miss Bara wears fifty distinctively different costumes, many of which are distinctive of the period." One newspaper columnist wrote, "Theda is Cleopatra physically and temperamentally. Words can hardly describe the wondrous costumes." Theda furnished and designed all of her costumes. Many of them bared the contours of her body and consisted of see-through netting made creatively from asbestos (not a material that would be used today!).

The history of Cleopatra as queen of Egypt until her sovereignty was overthrown by Octavius was recreated in California. A panoramic barge scene shot to recreate ships on the Nile was filmed at the mouth of Upper Newport Bay in Newport Beach, California. Set decorator George James Hopkins designed the famous city Alexandria and the exterior of Cleopatra's palace. These spectacular sets were built just below the Dover Shore cliffs. Thousands of spectators gathered on the cliffs to view the action as director Edwards, mounted on his horse, called for action. Theda's palace, an authentic reproduction of the original, was built near Dover Drive in Newport Beach. It included a stone platform leading down to the water's edge, so that when she landed from her barge, she wouldn't get her feet wet. Theda, attired in a robe of gold and with the symbol of Isis worn as a headpiece, can be seen in the movie entering the elaborate and gorgeous ornamental chariot drawn by four plumed white horses.

Theda as Cleopatra, from the film, *Cleopatra*, 1917 (Stout Collection).

The queen's fleet, manned by Egyptian warriors, floated in the water. Theda's elaborately decorated eighty-foot barge, followed by 29 ships (with each ship manned by 60 oarsmen), sailed towards Balboa Island. Scenes of the Battle of Actium were filmed in the channels off of Balboa Island and Little Island. While Theda floated on the lead barge, she dropped grapes from her bosom into her mouth. The censors thought that this scene was outrageous. Thousands of extras knelt before Cleopatra in homage at the slough of the Los Angeles River near Long Beach. The slough, filled with reeds and rushes, was a setting representative of the Nile.

When the censors viewed *Cleopatra*, they requested major cuts on the grounds that the story was immoral and it glorified the acts of Cleopatra as vicious.

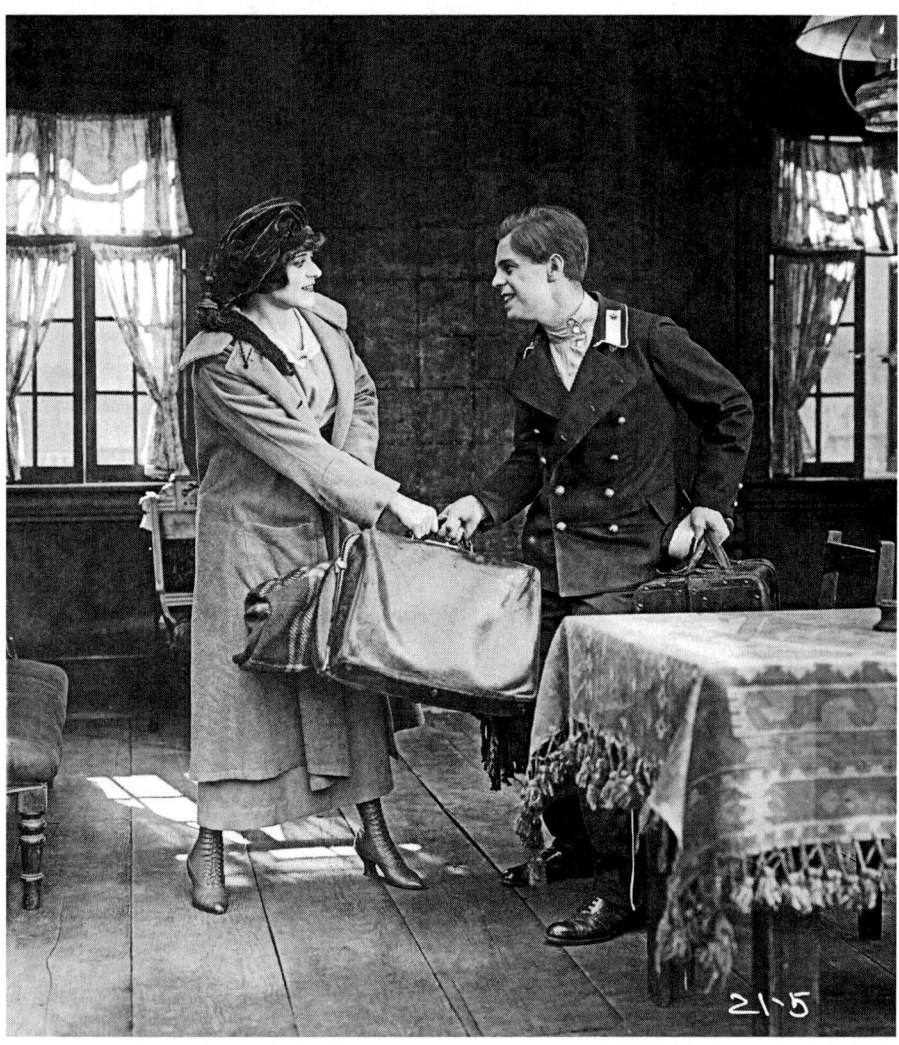

Theda as Lisza and Hector V. Sarno as the Revolutionist in *The Rose of Blood*, 1917 (Stout Collection).

The Rose of Blood

The Rose of Blood, directed by J. Gordon Edwards and authored by Bernard McConville and Richard Ordynski, was released on November 5, 1917. Ordynski, a former manager of Max Reinhardt's world-famous Deutsches Theatre in Berlin, wrote the Russian romance story depicting the pre-revolutionary crisis in Russia. The plot was a dramatic tragedy set during the time when the main outdoor sports were hunting and being hunted by anarchists. Ordynski is seen in the leading role of Vassea while Theda plays Lisza, the anarchist wife of a prince. Even though a princess, she is an ally of the revolutionists. She hunts and assassinates enemies of the people, always leaving a red rose behind. Tragically, she is ordered to kill her husband. She chooses to die with her prince.

The Rose of Blood was censored for fear that it might inspire American citizens to overthrow the government. It did get good reviews from several sources.

Du Barry

Du Barry, directed by J. Gordon Edwards, was released on December 30, 1917. The story was adapted for film by Adrian Johnson from the novel *Madame du Barry* by Alexandre Dumas.

Madame Du Barry (Theda) is the mistress of Louis XV (Charles Clary). Despite being

Theda as Madame du Barry, from the film *Du Barry*, 1917 (Stout Collection).

born of lower class status, she dominates Louis XV with her charm. Men became fascinated with Du Barry, enabling her to gain power over them. As she attains the status that she seeks, she begins to squander wealth to gratify her elegant desires. At the age of 50, Du Barry is executed by guillotine.

Du Barry was filmed at Fox's Edendale Studio where numerous beautiful and exotic scenes were created. Experts were consulted to reproduce in detail the scenes and costumes of the Louis XV period. With the help of George Hopkins, Theda's dresses became some of the most remarkable features of the film. Theda is mostly remembered with the adornment of a coiffed snowy wig and long full gown. It was reported in the newspapers that no one other than Theda could grasp and portray the character and psychology of Madame Du Barry.

It has been reported that the Fox version of *Du Barry* was not historically accurate; but that accuracy was sacrificed for high entertainment in the theaters.

1918

The Forbidden Path

The Forbidden Path, a romantic love story with a series of heart-throbbing situations, was directed by J. Gordon Edwards. Theda, as Mary Lynde, is a New York City tenement girl. Felix Benavente is commissioned to paint a portrait of the Madonna for a church. Felix sees Mary and asks her to be the model. Mary's father casts her from his home when he discovers his daughter's relationship with Felix's friend Robert Sinclair. Sinclair coerces young Mary to live with him in his mountain lodge. After she gives birth to their child, he casts her aside. When the baby dies, she sinks into despair and seeks revenge upon Sinclair.

While filming *The Forbidden Path*, Theda received a telegram with the following request:

> The 158th Infantry Regiment selected you for its Godmother by unanimous vote today. This regiment, composed of Arizona men, is all sincere admirers of you. Mary Pickford has adopted the 143rd Artillery Regiment here. We

Theda as Madame Du Barry (Stout Collection).

will be greatly disappointed if you turn us down. Please wire your acceptance at once.

About this time, Theda's three-year contract with Fox ended. She formed her own production company and contracted with Fox as dis-

Hugh Thompson as Robert Sinclair with Theda as Mary Lynde in *The Forbidden Path*, 1918 (Stout Collection).

tributors. Each film produced by her company was identifiable by the slogan "A Theda Bara Super Production" included underneath every title.

The Soul of Buddha

The first Theda Bara Super Production, *The Soul of Buddha*, was released on April 21, 1918. It was written by Theda, directed by J. Gor-

Florence Martin as Mrs. Romaine and Theda as Bava in *The Soul of Buddha*, 1918 (Stout Collection).

Albert Roscoe as Captain Paul Winchester and Theda as Maria Valverda in *Under the Yoke*, 1918 (Stout Collection).

don Edwards and filmed at Fort Lee, New Jersey. Theda, inspired by the sensational story of Mata Hari, wrote the screenplay while traveling via train from California to New York City. She handed the manuscript to William Fox upon arrival.

The Soul of Buddha introduces the audience to Bava, the beautiful daughter of a Javanese widow. Bava worships Buddha and is consecrated as a sacred dancer by Ysora, the high priest of the temple. Ysora is secretly in love with Bava. At a festival, Bava meets the English major Sir John Dare and elopes with him as the clock strikes midnight. Ysora follows them and swears vengeance. Sir John is cashiered from the army for his escapade. Bava then leaves her husband and makes her appearance as a dancer before the footlights in Paris. On the evening of her stage debut, Bava's husband comes to seek reconciliation, and at his wife's feet he kills himself. Ysora is disguised as a Buddha idol in the scene of the dance. Ysora comes to life and kills Bava before the audience. The film received mixed reviews.

Under the Yoke

The next Theda Bara Super Production, *Under the Yoke*, was also directed by J. Gordon Edwards. It was released on June 9, 1918.

Theda as Maria Valverda, a Spanish flirt, appears willful but adorable. She risks everything to save the life of a fighting American cavalryman and his troops. She becomes the victim of a cruel and coldblooded plot. The movie takes place in the Philippines during the American occupation. The soldiers are part of a regiment that went to teach the virtues and glories of self-government.

More than ten men were injured during the filming at Fox Studios in California when caissons and cannons overturned during a battle scene. Many picture magazines declared *Under the Yoke* a major triumph for Theda.

Salome

Theda arrived in San Bernardino, California, on February 8, 1918, on the Santa Fe Overland train to film *Salome*. The film was released on August 10. J. Gordon Edwards again was selected to direct. G. Raymond Nye played the part of King Herod, and Alan Roscoe portrayed John the Baptist.

Thousands of people were employed by Fox to build ancient Jerusalem. Details were reproduced from original biblical prints. George James Hopkins was hired as set decorator. The Jaffa Gate, the streets and buildings adjacent to Herod's Palace, the king's throne room, the tomb of Prince David, and Salome's boudoir were constructed. Cities were built and destroyed. For Herod's birthday feast, Theda (as Salome) recreated the Dance of the Seven Veils that won Salome the head of John the Baptist. There were desert scenes with camels, chariots, and battles.

Theda as Salome from the film *Salome*, 1918 (Stout Collection).

These scenes were recreated on locations in Yucaipa and Beaumont, California, utilizing 5,000 people and 2,800 animals. Theda's psychological interpretation of Salome followed that of the Jewish historian Josephus. Theda considered the role of the Judean princess of passion a great achievement in her career.

The National Board of Review of Motion Pictures reported that Theda's *Salome* was "a serious and dignified portrayal. It is imaginative with historical value and a powerful story. It is presented in a way that should rank with the best screen productions."

The film presentation was without climatic drama and carefully edited to satisfy the censor boards. Yet still there were cities that censored it to preserve purity.

When a Woman Sins

The Theda Bara Super Production *When a Woman Sins* was released on September 28, 1918. Beta Brueil wrote the story about Lillian, a young nurse to the lecherous Mortimer West (Josef Swickard).

Lillian falls in love with Mortimer's son (Albert Roscoe), a divinity student. The story continues to twist and turn until Lillian leaves and becomes a dancer notorious for her beautiful dresses. Lillian is seen in a mass of splendor and glitter dancing in a theater. (One article stated, "The Dance of Passion, the Broadway Revels, and the Banquet of Death were all outstanding scenes in the film.") Lillian, now named Poppea, is still in love with the young clergyman. She decides to end it all by auctioning herself off to the highest bidder and then drinking poison. However, she receives a bunch of lilies from the young priest and this changes everything.

The She-Devil

The Theda Bara Super Production *The She-Devil*, written by George James Hopkins and directed by J. Gordon Edwards, was

Theda as Lillian in *When a Woman Sins*, 1918 (Stout Collection).

Theda as Lolette in *The She-Devil*, 1918 (Stout Collection).

released on November 10, 1918. It was filmed in Spain and France by the Fox Company.

The She-Devil is about the love affair of Lolette (Theda), a beautiful woman without a conscience. A Spanish girl, she lives in a mountain home above Seville. Maurice (Albert Roscoe), an artist, encounters Lolette, who becomes his guide and shows him locations to paint. Lolette falls in love with Maurice. However, Maurice plans to leave by coach to return to Paris without her. A bandit named Tiger (George McDaniel) has been lusting after Lolette. In one scene, Lolette jumps upon the back of Tiger as he rides his horse and she steals some jewels and loot from him. They come upon the coach carrying Maurice as it travels from the top of a mountain to a valley. Lolette escapes from Tiger on horseback and intercepts the coach. She climbs aboard with the driver. As the coach descends, it gains momentum and careens from side to side with Lolette holding on for dear life. At a turn, it looks as if the horses, coach, and passengers will go over the side. (Edwards selected a very picturesque road in Spain for this scene.) Lolette follows Maurice to Paris.

According to the *Reading Eagle* (January 1, 1919), Theda remarked after the ride was over, "When the stagecoach went out of control with the horses racing down the mountain, my heart simply stopped beating. It surely was an exciting experience. At times we were going so fast it took my breath away. When I set foot on the ground again I sent up a prayer for my safe delivery. I should not want to do it over again!"

1919

The Light

The Light, another Theda Bara Super Production, was released on January 12, 1919. The story was written by Luther Reed and Brett Page. Theda starred as Blanchette Dumond, a wicked woman in Paris. A sculptor sees Blanchette and feels that there must be some goodness behind such a beautiful face. While he gazes upon her he sees a halo above her. He doesn't see that she is the wickedest woman in Paris. Blanchette poses for him and he creates a statue of the Madonna. She dances with a gunman of Paris. Together they reenact their street life in pantomime to a tango. As she dances, she is strenuously embraced and acts out fear; at the same time she shows him devotion. She elopes with the gunman and as they depart she sees the sculptor who has been

Theda as Blanchette Dumond in *The Light*, 1919 (Stout Collection).

suddenly blinded. As she gazes at him on the street she sees the light through the blind sculptor.

The Light was filmed at the studio at Fort Lee, New Jersey, and in New Orleans, Louisiana.

G. Raymond Nye as Von Rohn and Theda as Marie Lohr in *When Men Desire*, 1919 (Stout Collection).

When Men Desire

The Theda Bara Super Production *When Men Desire* was released on March 9, 1919, a mere two months after *The Light*. Written by J. Searle Dawley and directed by J. Gordon Edwards, the film depicts the adventures of a woman who would not sin. War is the somber setting for the story. Theda plays Marie Lohr, a shy American country girl of German parentage who studies music in Germany. She tries to get to America. The German officials beset her with difficulties: The Fatherland is not willing to let this girl out of its clutches. Marie falls in love with Robert Stedman, a plucky American aviator. This arouses the jealousy of her German suitor Major von Rohn, who makes every effort to keep the lovers apart. Von Rohn tries to hold up her passport and to contrive conditions whereby Marie will be detained in Germany and possibly fall into his hands. Marie is forced to administer the death blow with a gleaming dagger. (Theda uses the dagger that was given to her by Pancho Villa.)

In New York City, a sign in front of a theater read, "Censors refuse to allow us to advertise the name of this picture!" The management boldly displayed the name Theda Bara on the marquee, followed by: "Regular Theda Bara Picture, Want To See It?"

The following poem written by Theda appeared in the *Herald Tribune* on April 18, 1919, a month after the release of *When Men Desire*:

Theda Bara Takes Flight in Aeroplane in *When Men Desire*

No more cozy corner or sheltered garden nook for modern lovers!
They are as passers, as the old buggy and Romeo's ladder.
The romance of the future will take place in the sky
Aero planes––that's all!

How much more poetical I love you will sound up in the clouds
than it has sounded heretofore in the subway train or on the roadside.
Romeo will come knocking at the skyscraper window of his love's
apartment and bear her away into the heavens.

Close to the moon and stars they will make their eternal vows.
And when they elope, they will flee via the trackless expanse of the sky,
where neither detectives nor erratic fathers can follow them.
I've been in an aero plane, and that is why I know.

I did not go with my Romeo, but at least I soared from earth with a make
 believe Romeo.
For I took this first aero plane flight for a scene in *When Men Desire*,
where I flee to happiness with my motion picture hero.
And all the time I could imagine two real lovers flying the way we make
 believe lovers were flying.

The earth below looked so small and insignificant! I felt like a giant who
 could pick up the houses
in his hands and crush the ant-like people and tiny houses under his
 thumb.
I felt big and all-powerful, as if I and my companion were the only beings
 in the universe—
an ideal feeling for people who are in love.

I could imagine how cozy they would feel in their whizzing bird machine,
with the great lonely heavens as the only witness to their courting.
No fear of little brother spying on their first kiss from behind the
 curtains.
No fear of an automobile searchlight, flashing its telltale rays upon the
 privacy of the park bench!
No fear of having to shout out their love to all the world from the back
 seat on top of a bus!
No fear of being discovered by prying busybodies, or of being disturbed
 by the arrival of a beau!

The Romeo and Juliet of the aero plane can scorn the world, for they have the heavens all to themselves.
A prophecy that within the next decade every lover who has enough pennies saved
up will invest them in a flivver of a flying machine.

See if I'm not right!

The Siren's Song

The Siren's Song, another Theda Bara Super Production, was released on May 4, 1919. This picture was released 56 days after *When Men Desire*. At this point in her career, the production schedules must have been harrowing for Theda. However, she continued to try to meet deadlines along with the rest of the staff. J. Gordon Edwards was again called upon to direct. Charles Kenyon was chosen to write the script.

It is a cautionary tale of deceit: A hypocrite can retire behind the mask of goodness and trust that no one will discover his deceit. Marie

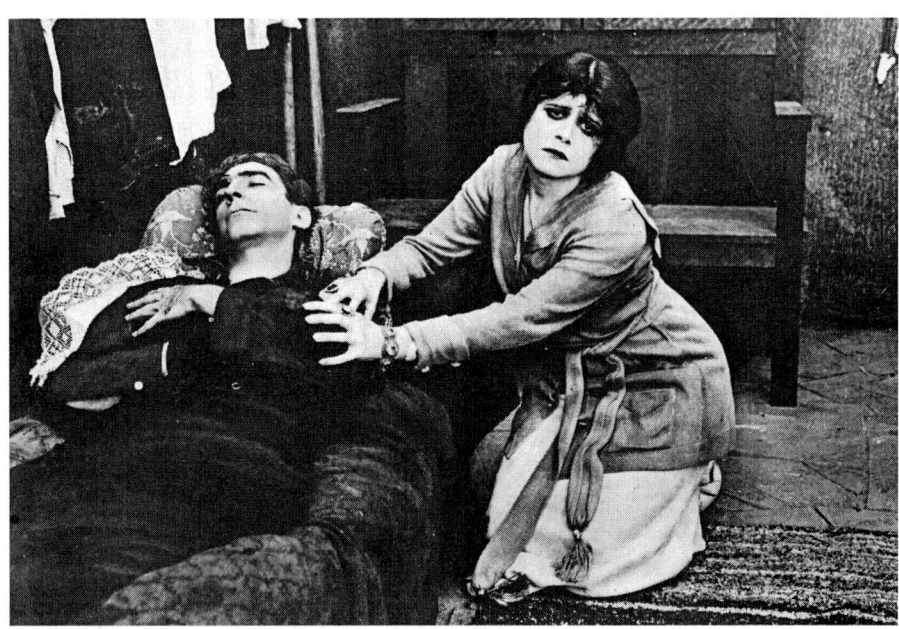

Theda as Marie Bernais with an unidentified actor in *The Siren's Song*, 1919 (Stout Collection).

11. The Films

Bernais, played by Theda, is the daughter of a Breton lighthouse keeper (Al Fremont). Her conservative father thinks his daughter's beautiful singing voice is that of a siren. He wants her to marry Nieppe (Lee Shumway), a minister. Instead, her voice teacher takes her to Paris. Marie becomes successful as a singer and falls in love with wealthy

William B. Davidson as the Reverend Winthrop Stark and Theda as Princess Zara in *A Woman There Was*, 1919 (Stout Collection).

Gaspard Prevost (Alan Roscoe). Nieppe finds her and insists that she return to her village and sing for the soldiers. Upon her arrival home, her father, in a fit of anger, has a heart attack and dies. Discovering that Nieppe is lustful, Marie realizes that she left the man she loves because of the deceit of another.

A Woman There Was

The next Theda Bara Super Production, *A Woman There Was* (released on June 1, 1919), was an adaptation of George James Hopkins' *Creation's Tears*. J. Gordon Edwards directed Theda as savage Zara, the princess of a South Seas island tribe. Supporting actors were William B. Davidson, Robert Elliott, Claude Payton and John Ardizoni.

An old ragged schooner was bought for the film and used in the waters around Cape Florida. Crowds of spectators flocked to the area north of the Miami Beach Casino to watch the filming. Another location north of the army ballistic station was used for the filming. Here spectators were able to watch Theda, dressed in a skirt made of long shredded wheat strands, play the role of Princess Zara. In the story, Zara is a woman of fire who defies her tribe and gives her life to save an American missionary to whom she has offered her love.

While filming *A Woman There Was*, the schooner took on water and began to sink. All of the cast and crew members were forced to swim ashore. Some of the crew could not swim. All survived except one. The Theda Bara Production Company was not faulted; however, Theda was devastated by the loss of a crew member. It brought home to everyone the unforeseen dangers and risks associated with the business of making films.

Kathleen Mavourneen

Kathleen Mavourneen, a Theda Bara Super Production, proved to be quite controversial. It was released on August 19, 1919. Charles Brabin directed and wrote the screenplay based on Dion Boucicault's play of the same name.

The film opens with the old Irish poem in subtitles telling the love story of a poor Irish peasant girl, Kathleen. In the story, Kathleen

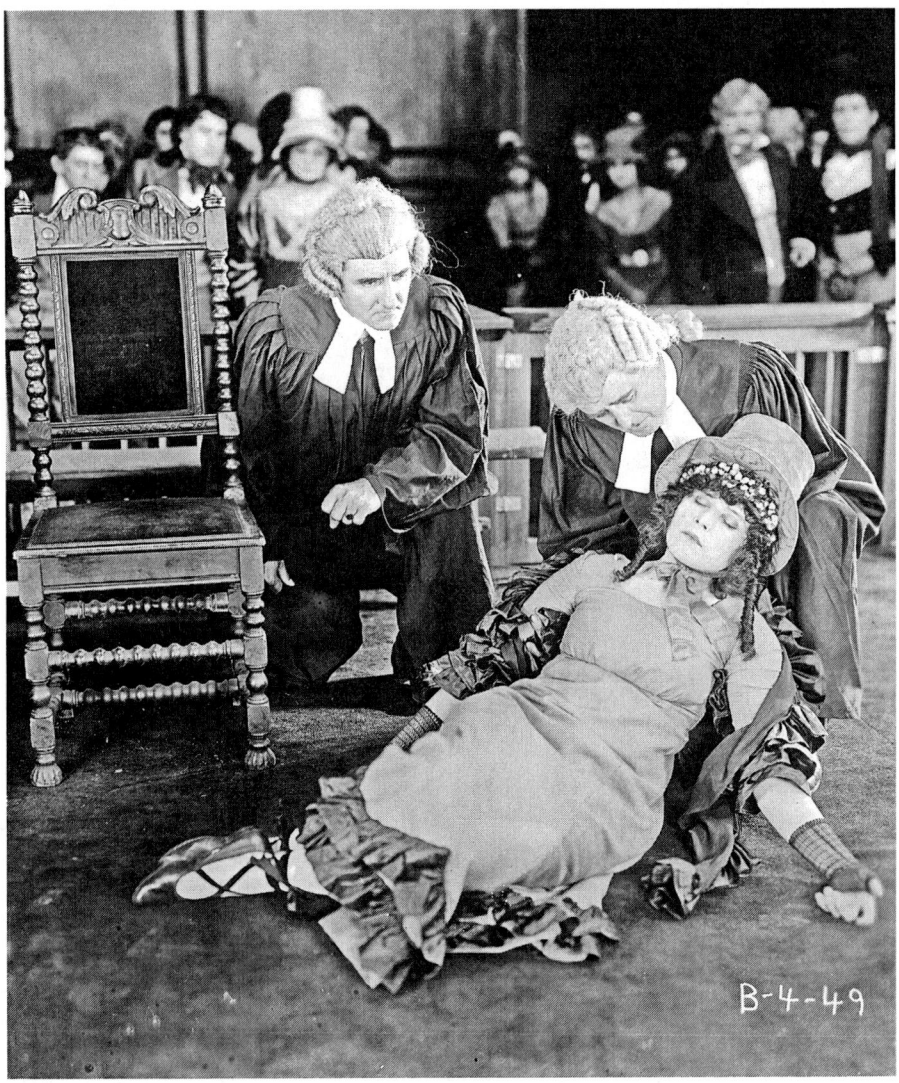

Theda as Kathleen attended to by unidentified court officials in *Kathleen Mavourneen*, 1919 (photograph provided by Bruce Calvert, Silents are Golden website).

(Theda) is engaged to blacksmith Terence O'Moore (Raymond McKee). While dancing at the Donnybrook fair, Kathleen attracts the attention of the Squire of Traise (Marc McDermott). He's the fiancé of Lady Clancarthy (Marcia Harris), who is not nearly as pretty as Kathleen.

When Kathleen rebuffs the squire, he threatens to evict her family from his land unless she marries him. Kathleen, as she worries and considers accepting the proposal, falls asleep by the fire. She dreams that she accepts the squire's proposal and they marry. However, after several years, the squire tires of Kathleen's lowly status and plots to have her killed. Terence learns of the squire's intentions and saves Kathleen but, while saving her, he kills a man. The squire testifies against Terence and he is convicted of murder and hangs. Suddenly Kathleen is awakened by Terence and released from her horrendous dream. Kathleen is saved from a life that could have been and she accepts Terence's proposal of marriage.

One scene was replicated from a painting which depicted the interior of an old farmhouse with pigeons fluttering in the rafters, with a sow and a litter of pigs in the parlor. There were panoramic views of Ireland's countryside and picturesque cottages and castles

Theda loved the role of Kathleen. Happy *not* to be playing another vamp role, she played the role lightheartedly and sometimes comically.

However, Theda's happiness regarding the film was short-lived. A February 9, 1920, news release from the United Press reported that a mob of angry theatergoers at the Sun Movie Theater in San Francisco rushed the film operator to get the reels of the movie. The operator was held against the wall and the projector was demolished. The riot was sparked partly from the showing of pigs in the parlor of an Irish home. Another, more serious reason for the outrage was the fact that Theda Bara, a Jewish actress, was chosen to play the role of Kathleen. Riots broke out across the country and in Europe, and the film was pulled from theaters. In Ireland, stink bombs were rolled down the aisles of one theater. It was a senselessly cruel situation but Theda weathered the storm. Nothing could diminish her happiness over the fact that she and Charles Brabin had become close while making the film.

There were two earlier versions of *Kathleen Mavourneen*. Brabin, working for the Edison Company, wrote and directed a one-reel version starring Mary Fuller, Marc McDermott and Augustus Phillips. Herbert Brenon, working under the auspices of the Independent Moving Pictures Company of America, made a three-reel version starring Jane Fearnley and William E. Shay. Both films were released on the same day in 1913.

Brabin and Brenon both considered filmmaking a graphic art.

11. The Films

They spared no expense creating scenes true to their historical eras. Brabin was especially known to portray scenes in exact detail, which he derived from studying the scenes in a tableau vivant. The tableau vivant is an art form whereby a group of actors pose for a scene as if they were in a photograph. Details and props are true to the period. Brabin would often use photographs to study the details of an era.

Theda as Fleurette Sackton in *La Belle Russe*, 1919 (Stout Collection).

La Belle Russe

The Theda Bara Super Production *La Belle Russe* (released September 21, 1919) was based on a play written by David Belasco. The film was directed and co-written by Charles Brabin. It is a gripping story of conflicts between identical twin sisters La Belle Russe, the wicked one, and Fleurette, the nice one. Fleurette, a dancer, is married to a nobleman. La Belle Russe lives the life of a courtesan. She tries to take over the identity of Fleurette. Theda plays both sisters. Cinematographer George W. Lane used sensational double exposure effects. With the use of mirrors and camera effects, Theda was able to portray the twin sisters on film face to face before the camera at the same time.

The ballet costume designed by Theda was made of swan feathers and stitched together by hand. An exquisite Gobelin wall tapestry is seen in the film.

Theda as Olga Dolan in *The Lure of Ambition*, 1919 (Stout Collection).

The Lure of Ambition

The Lure of Ambition was released on November 16, 1919. The story was written by Julia Burnham; the screenwriter and director was Edmund Lawrence.

This is the story of poor and wretched Olga Dolan (Theda). Working as a stenographer at a posh New York hotel, Olga meets the Honorable Cyril Ralston, an Englishman who offers to improve her life. She is led to believe that Ralston will eventually marry her; Ralston has no such intention because he is married. He leaves New York and returns to England. Olga, incensed, follows him. Eventually Olga meets and marries the Duke of Rutledge, who steals her heart.

After six years of nearly nonstop and grueling work for William Fox, Theda walked away. Fox, on J. Gordon Edwards' advice, replaced Theda with Betty Blythe, but Blythe could never draw the crowds that Theda had. And by the time Theda left Fox, the era of gullible moviegoers was mostly at an end. Movies were becoming more sophisticated and so were the audiences.

Theda Bara as Carolyn Knollys with Evelyn Selbie on set of *The Unchastened Woman*, 1926. The child actor is unidentified (Stout Collection).

Theda, after some well-deserved time off, looked around for her next project. She was finally free of Fox, but the security of knowing that a movie would be found for her was gone. She was on her own in a Hollywood that was changing very fast. There was even talk of making movies with sound. Theda had never uttered a word in her films.

Finally she was approached in 1920 by a Broadway producer to star in *The Blue Flame*. Theda read the script and accepted the offer. Little did she know of the problems that were in store for her.

1925

The Unchastened Woman

The Blue Flame tour, which followed its run at the Schubert Theater, ended on January 1, 1921. Theda would not work again until a small company, Chadwick Pictures, offered her a starring role in their upcoming movie *The Unchastened Woman*.

Released on November 16, 1925, the photoplay was directed by James Young. Louis K. Anspacher wrote the play and Douglas Z. Doty adapted it to the screen. *The Unchastened Woman* most likely had the simplest storyline of any of Theda's films. Pregnant Carolyn Knollys (Theda) is happily married to Hubert Knollys (Wyndham Standing). When Carolyn finds her husband cheating with another woman, she leaves him and travels to Europe. The baby is born and Carolyn becomes a very popular society woman in Venice. She attracts many suitors but decides to return to America. Hubert learns that Carolyn was very popular in Venice when some of her suitors follow her to America. He suddenly realizes what he has lost and Carolyn takes him back. In one of the last scenes in the movie, Hubert picks up his child and the family huddles together in their newfound happiness. This film is the last of Theda's feature silent films and one of her three remaining full-length existing films.

1926

Madame Mystery

Shortly after the release of *The Unchastened Woman*, Theda was approached by Hal Roach to do a series of short comedies. Theda had

Theda as Madame Mysterieux in *Madame Mystery*, 1926 (Stout Collection).

decided that comedy was her forte and she was interested in Roach's offer. The film that Roach had in mind, *Madame Mystery*, was shot in a short amount of time and Theda received a nice compensation for her efforts.

The story line was quite ridiculous; it was camp to the max. Madame Mystereaux, a secret agent, travels on board a ship with her special cargo, a helium nitrate bomb. Thieves attempt to steal the bomb and in the melee, one thief swallows it. It doesn't explode but, being helium, it elevates him to great heights. He floats off into the sky with his partner spy clinging to his leg. In addition, the bomb expands him to an atrocious size. The story ends when a passing pelican pecks the thief's stomach and he explodes. The story is so camp that it is hard to imagine Theda Bara in such a role. But Roach was shrewd enough to dress Theda well in the movie. As has always been the case, fans came to see Theda, the great star of the silents. Theda was not totally pleased with the final results so she cancelled her remaining contract with Roach. *Madame Mystery* was Theda's swan song. She always stated that she was interested in making other films, but nothing materialized. The body of work that gave us the first great siren of the screen was complete. Theda spent the rest of her life mixing in Hollywood society along with her husband Charles, who directed until his retirement in 1934.

Theda did have a cameo in *45 Minutes from Hollywood*, a two-reel silent film with Stan Laurel and Oliver Hardy. It was produced and written by Hal Roach and released on December 26, 1926. This was a short comedy about a young man, visiting Hollywood on family business, who meets Theda Bara. Theda did not actually act in the charming little film; her brief appearance was from previously shot footage.

12

Charles Brabin

Uncle Charlie and Me

Uncle Charlie always had a Tums in his pocket and maybe a nickel. He wasn't broke. He just lived happily under the thumb of Theda Bara. He was a very patient person. On one of my first visits, I brought with me a book, *We Look and See*, that I read to him. However, he did not have the patience to hear me read this book aloud over and over! He quickly reached for *A Child's Garden of Verses* by Robert Louis Stevenson. As I read it, I stumbled over the words so Uncle Charlie would describe a perfect picture of what I was reading.

It was from this exchange of imaginations with Uncle Charlie that I learned to enjoy reading the poems of Poe, Longfellow, Twain, and Shakespeare.

Uncle Charlie was a trustworthy man. I could tell him my thoughts and he would keep a secret! Over a period of time as I grew older and could understand, he shared with me his deepest thoughts about his life.

When Uncle Charlie was hired in 1908 as stage manager at Edison Studios (located at Decatur Avenue and Olive Place in the Bronx), he truly felt honored. The building was built of concrete and iron with a glass roof for proper lighting for filming indoors. He said that he was so enthusiastic because Thomas Edison was at the helm of the new studio. Also, there was talk of multi-reel films being made in the near future and Uncle Charlie believed that this was a cutting edge opportunity. He rented a room just a block or so from the studio. He always clocked out his time card at the regular hour, but he did not stop working until his chores for the day were done.

Uncle Charlie was in charge of sets and props which had to be changed frequently. A screening stage did not remain idle! He said that each filming was really an experiment. Once a director had finished filming a scene, the stage was immediately made ready for the next film. Organization was the key to keeping track of the items for each scene. The studio was run like a factory so that many films could be shot on the same day. This also allowed actors to be used in different films under the supervision of other directors on the same day.

The films at that time could not be longer than 300 feet or eighteen minutes in duration. The studio was equipped with its own laboratory. Once the film was completed, it was sent to the Edison Company in New Jersey to be reviewed and approved by Thomas Edison.

Uncle Charlie, as stage manager, had the opportunity to observe and learn from Edwin S. Porter, the co-inventor (with Edison) of the motion picture camera. He explained that the films were viewed in brown and white or black and white; true colors were of no importance. Staged sets were painted in various shades of blacks, browns and whites. James Searle Dawley directed *Fireside Reminisces* in 1908; Uncle Charlie's description was so vivid I could envision him as being part of the working team.

In 1909, Marc McDermott signed a contract with Edison Films. This marked the beginning of a lifelong friendship between McDermott and Uncle Charlie. They collaborated as producers on many fine films. McDermott was born in New South Wales and educated at the Jesuit College of Sydney, Australia. He and Uncle Charlie were six feet tall and aristocratic in manner. Both had an abundance of creative ideas and they often shared British humor. McDermott was a handsome natural actor with grace and charm. Uncle Charlie said that his early days at Edison Studios were some of the most fun times of his life.

Charles Brabin (Stout Collection).

Uncle Charlie's face would light up when he talked about the filming of James S. Dawley's *Frankenstein*, starring Charles Ogle as the monster and August Phillips as Frankenstein. He said that some of his unique ideas for the scenes were incorporated into the film. I could tell that Uncle Charlie was very proud of his work. While I watched the film with him, he would point to something and say, "I did that!"

A Christmas Carol, starring Marc McDermott as Scrooge, was released in 1910. "He became a star in demand," stated Uncle Charlie. In 1911, McDermott appeared as Thomas Jefferson in *The Declaration of Independence* with Robert Brower as Benjamin Franklin, Harry Linsom as John Adams, and Miriam Nesbitt as Mrs. John Adams. Both movies were filmed at Edison Studios.

By 1912, Uncle Charlie had experienced every part of filmmaking. Many of his early films are missing or forgotten, but many of the ones I saw, *I* haven't forgotten. In the early days of filming, Uncle Charlie filmed shorts on labor issues, manufacturing, and farming as well as travelogues. I remember a film about soil erosion during a heavy rain, with closeups of chunks of soil falling away from tree roots. Another film was about beavers building a dam. Some of these films were shown at my school because they were considered educational. An early fourteen-minute film directed by Uncle Charlie entitled *Hope* exists today in the University of California Berkeley Library. It is a Red Cross Seal story written by James Oppenheim.

Uncle Charlie, while pointing to his globe, would describe to me the places and experiences he encountered while filming for Edison Studios in England, Wales, the Thames Valley, Belgium, France, and Italy. He traveled with his first wife, Susette, Marc McDermott, Miriam Nesbitt, writer Bannister Merwin, and cameraman Oto Braufgam. They often encountered rudeness while traveling. Filming at that time was not considered a professional job. Brabin said, "Marc was always ready to do a ridiculous stunt in front of the camera. I regret that I encouraged him because it was very dangerous." Uncle Charlie spoke about the time when, after a long day of filming, he and the crew returned to the hotel very tired. The hotel management denied them rooms by stating, "We don't rent rooms to your sort of people. You will have to go elsewhere." Uncle Charlie said, "My wife, Susette, was so insulted that she wanted to go home."

Uncle Charlie explained to me the importance of courtesy. He did this by reading to me a poem entitled "Craven (Mobile Bay, 1864)," written by Sir Henry Newbolt. He said, "The poem tells the story of an American hero of courtesy." The poem, in part, is as follows:

> Over the turret, shut in his iron-clad tower,
> Craven was conning his ship through smoke and flame;
> Gun to gun he had battered the fort for an hour,
> Now was the time for a charge to end the game.
>
> There lay the narrowing channel, smooth and grim,
> A hundred deaths beneath it, and never a sign;
> There lay the enemy's ships, and sink or swim
> The flag was flying, and he was head of the line.
>
> The fleet behind was jamming; the monitor hung
> Beating the stream; the roar for a moment hushed,
> Craven spoke to the pilot; slow she swung;
> Again he spoke, and right for the foe she rushed.
>
> Into the narrowing channel, between the shore
> And the sunk torpedoes lying in treacherous rank;
> She turned but a yard too short; a muffled roar,
> A mountainous wave, and she rolled, righted, and sank.
>
> Over the manhole, up in the iron-clad tower,
> Pilot and Captain met as they turned to fly:
> The hundredth part of a moment seemed an hour,
> For one could pass to be saved, and one must die.
>
> They stood like men in a dream: Craven spoke,
> Spoke as he lived and fought, with a Captain's pride,
> "After you, Pilot." The pilot woke,
> Down the ladder he went, and Craven died.
>
> All men praise the deed and the manner, but we—
> We set it apart from the pride that stoops to the proud,
> The strength that is supple to serve the strong and free,
> The grace of the empty hands and promises loud:
>
> Sidney thirsting, a humbler need to slake,
> Nelson waiting his turn for the surgeon's hand,
> Lucas crushed with chains for a comrade's sake,
> Outram coveting right before command:
>
> These were paladins, these were Craven's peers,
> These with him shall be crowned in story and song,
> Crowned with the glitter of steel and the glimmer of tears,
> Princes of courtesy, merciful, proud, and strong.

When Uncle Charlie finished reading the poem, he said, "I had such admiration for this man of courage and courtesy that I wrote a scenario based on the poem for filming. The man I speak of is your great-great grandfather Commodore Tunis Augustus Macdonough Craven, the captain who gave his life for the pilot John Collins to escape from the sinking USS *Tecumseh*."

12. Charles Brabin

Uncle Charlie was ready to direct the filming of the Battle of Mobile Bay on March 28, 1914, at the Edison Studios in the Bronx. The forts, wooden battleships, tugboats, launches, and monitors were in place, ready for the cameras to roll. According to the *New York Times*, on March 29, 1914, there were twelve men working in the early morning, painting the last twelve ocean waves on canvases representing the bay and ocean, when they heard the night watchman Daniel Collins call out "Fire!" The stage where the men were working quickly filled with thick black smoke and the men had difficulty finding their way out of the darkness. Suddenly the firemen appeared along with the general stage manager of Edison Films, John Collins. Collins, a brave man bearing the same name as Craven's pilot, raced into the burning building with his assistant. They were able to rescue some films and a few cameras just before the glass roof collapsed and the interior became engulfed in flames.

A motion picture depicting the Battle of Mobile Bay has never been made. The monitor *Tecumseh* has never been raised. A buoy swings to and fro with the tide in Mobile Bay. It marks the scene of Craven's duty, high courage, and courtesy. It also marks the place where he died.

Uncle Charlie moved to Hollywood in 1917 and joined Metro Pictures as a contract director. On August 6, 1918, it was reported in the *New York Times* that Charles J. Brabin, Edwin Carewe, Albert Capellani, John H. Collins, Herbert Blache, Wilfred Lucas, Ralph W. Ince, John Ince, Harry L. Franklin, E. Mason Hopper, and William S. Davis were at work on the company's multiple-reel productions. Many of these directors were unable to make a transition from silent films to talkies.

Uncle Charlie said that making a movie was a tremendous challenge. He also said that so much could go wrong, but sometimes the unexpected could turn into a great thing. Some of the best scenes would pile up on the cutting room floor before a film was finished. The directors had to deal with missing shots and missing segments.

In the early 1950s, there was a call to identify all of the films that had been made. By that time, many films had been destroyed, lost or forgotten. Uncle Charlie submitted many films that, at that time, could not be identified or accounted for. Records regarding the making of many early films could not be found. Neither could the films themselves be found. The only evidence of their existence was in newspaper accounts or by word of mouth. It was a sad state of affairs for these early films.

I remember scenes of Marc McDermott and Charles Ogle on a chase and a struggle on top of a moving train. There was also a segment where McDermott and Ogle, as window washers in a struggle, nearly fell from a New York City skyscraper. These segments were inserted into televised commercials in the 1950s. The films no longer existed, and the commercial segments are all that is left of these films.

It was during this time of compiling the films and credits that phone calls were made to gather information. Past friendships were renewed. Once, Lionel Barrymore came for dinner. After the guests had settled down with a cocktail, Mr. Barrymore expressed that he had wanted to visit Charles and Theda for a very long time, but he had not gotten around to doing so. Mr. Barrymore said that he wanted to apologize for the humiliation that Uncle Charlie endured while directing 1932's *Rasputin and the Empress*. Uncle Charlie and Mr. Barrymore immediately began to laugh as they reminisced about all the bickering. Mr. Barrymore began to get heated while blaming his sister for some of the problems. Uncle Charlie said, "I just couldn't film her at that angle in that dress!" Mr. Barrymore then looked directly at me and said, "I come from a family of stage actors and when we get together we never seem to get along. My sister would not take direction. She once called Mr. Mayer and then had him fired. I want you to remember that your Uncle Charlie was not at fault. He unfortunately became the victim of a family squabble." All in all, it was an enjoyable evening. During dinner, Uncle Charlie and Mr. Barrymore never stopped reminiscing. There was much conversation starting with, "Do you remember when…."

It seems odd to me now that I was there for this evening. I can only determine that I was always included. I remember Mr. Barrymore's eloquent speech as he described how much he enjoyed composing music and drawing. His manner, when he spoke about his work, truly implied that he had found fulfillment through his creations.

Uncle Charlie said that he enjoyed his life but there was a lesson to be learned. He told me, "Many times during one's lifetime, what you expect to turn out doesn't always turn out the way that you think it will. It is difficult to foresee the future in a rapidly changing world. I made decisions based on what I knew at the time." After he thought for a moment, he said, "If I had my life to do over, I would not change anything."

Uncle Charlie was known amongst his peers for his imaginative use of double and triple exposures, and his ability to create eerie effects with mechanical contrivances and unusual lighting. The people he knew and the people he worked with remained his friends throughout his life.

The Early Years

Charles Brabin was born on April 17, 1882, in Liverpool, England. His father owned a butcher business and the name Brabin still remained engraved on a building in Liverpool in the 1950s. Charles graduated with honors from St. Francis Xavier's College in Liverpool, a strict Jesuit men's college. At this school Charles gained his life's interest in architecture, history and culture. Charles' first desire was to be an architect. He came to Chicago where he worked as a butcher in the early 1900s. It was in Chicago that he became inspired by the life of President Abraham Lincoln.

Brabin began his film career as an actor. His long legs enabled him to present a likeness to President Lincoln so he performed a monologue in road shows, schools, and on stage entitled *The Life of Lincoln.* His prologue included the Gettysburg Address. As a stage actor, Brabin was cast in 1904 in a British musical, *The Medal and the Maid* with Ruth Vincent. He was hired by Edison Studios as stage manager in 1908. Brabin lived frugally while reinvesting seventy-five percent of every weekly paycheck into purchasing stock shares in the Motion Pictures Patents Company (MPPC).

In 1910, Brabin and

Charles Brabin (Stout Collection).

Edwin August, starring as themselves, created the film *Love and the Law*, based on Charles Dickens' novel. In 1911, Edwin S. Porter directed *The Strike at the Mines* starring Charles Ogle (the first Frankenstein in 1910), Nancy Avril, Frank McGlynn Sr., Marc McDermott and Brabin. Brabin's first picture as a director was the first propaganda picture, *The Usurer's Grip* (1910), which exposed the nefarious methods of money-lending sharks. He appeared in his own written work, *His First Commission* (1911), as Abraham Lincoln.

In 1912, Brabin directed the first motion picture serial made in the United States, *What Happened to Mary*. It consisted of twelve monthly one-reel episodes and starred Mary Fuller, Marc McDermott, Charles Ogle and Herbert Yost. Brabin was praised for his photo realism with Marc McDermott as his leading man. McDermott was a handsome six-foot Shakespearean actor, and along with Mary Fuller, they became the popular stars of the day.

By the end of 1913, Charles had become an established producer. He married Susette Mosher on the evening of December 14, 1913. McDermott served as best man.

In order to film the ten-chapter *The Man Who Disappeared*, Brabin took a crew on location. This was to be the first-ever series which was planned to run concurrently in *Popular Magazine* and on the screen. In one episode, Brabin has Marc McDermott, as a fugitive, lie against a railroad track with handcuffs on his wrist with the links lying across the track. Brabin instructed that the train would roll past, crushing the links and setting McDermott free. The scene caught on camera was breathtaking! In another episode, Brabin took the crew to the top of an unfinished building with a panoramic view of the East River and the Woolworth and Singer Towers. Brabin captured on film the scene of a fight between one actor and McDermott on a rickety girder hanging on the outside of the building. The series was released in movie houses beginning in April 1914.

Brabin's wife Susette thought that Charles should get a respectable job. She became upset with Charles filming dangerous stunts for *The Man Who Disappeared*. Charles and Susette went for a rest at Brabin's vacation home in Nova Scotia. Susette liked it so much she never wanted to return to the city. The property had acreage so Susette started a refuge for ill-treated, sick and discarded animals from the fur trade. Charles assisted her in building a care facility and a separate home on the property.

12. Charles Brabin

By 1915, Edison Films was on the decline. The MPPC, known as the Edison Trust, came to an end when a federal court decision on October 1, 1915, ruled that their patents were a monopoly that restrained trade under the Sherman Antitrust Act. MPPC was officially terminated in 1918. Brabin's investment in MPPC became worthless.

Brabin completed the feature film *Vanity Fair* starring Minnie Madderm Fiske and transferred to Gilbert M. Anderson's Essanay Studios in Chicago. His wife Susette declined to live in Chicago. The marriage was terminated and Susette remained in Nova Scotia with her animal sanctuary. Charles retained the use of the main house. Susette lived at the sanctuary for the rest of her life.

At Essanay Studios, Brabin wrote the screenplay and directed the celebrated actor Henry B. Walthall in a haunting perspective into the life of Edgar Allan Poe. The photoplay, *The Raven*, was considered an achievement in imaginative cinema. He experimented with lighting techniques and became the first director to include text within the action in a silent film. The film was sensationalized by the use of a live raven that was borrowed from a zoo. Charles' *While New York Sleeps* (1920) was made up of three stories featuring the same actors in each story. It depicted corruption in New York City. At this time, Brabin was held in high esteem by his contemporaries for his scenario writing and as a director making popular films. Aside from his work in films, he also amassed considerable wealth with his conservative stock portfolio investments.

A secret wedding took place between Theda and Charles in Greenwich, Connecticut, on July 2, 1921. The marriage was not a rush decision. (Charles was now married to one wife by the church and married to Theda by the state.) They honeymooned in privacy at Brabin's charming English cottage retreat in Nova Scotia. They both were able to spend the entire summer away from the film industry and enjoy quiet time together. During this time, Theda became interested in protecting animals preyed on by the fur trade industry. Both she and Charles supported Susette and her sanctuary in protecting the fur trade animals.

While on her honeymoon, Theda was intrigued by a short story entitled "The Flower of the Flock," written by Jay Gelzer and published in the August 1921 issue of *Cosmopolitan Magazine*. She felt that it was a culturally important story with a psychological and dramatic theme about primitive life in the Blue Ridge Mountains. Theda prompted Charles to form his own company and use his own money to produce a low-budget film.

Theda read another article that emotionally inspired her. It was about Herbert Birch Kingston of Cleveland, Ohio, a candy company employee who wanted to bring happiness to the lives of orphans, shut-ins and others who were often neglected and forgotten. Theda was overwhelmed with Kingston's kindness. On October 8th she contacted him and requested a distribution of 10,000 boxes of candy to people in Cleveland hospitals. Every year thereafter she continued to have boxes of candy distributed on the third Saturday of October, "The Sweetest Day of the Year."

Brabin completed two successful films for Fox in 1922, *The Broadway Peacock* starring Pearl White and *The Lights of New York*, which was authored by Brabin. (This is not to be confused with the first all-talking film *Lights of New York*, which was released by Warner Brothers in 1922.) In 1923, Brabin went into production with *The Story of the Flock*, which eventually became known as *Driven*. Filming on location in the hills of Kentucky on a low budget, Brabin was able to produce the photoplay with his own money.

Driven is the story of a mother who assures the happiness of her youngest and most sensitive son by selling out her moonshiner husband and three brute hillbilly sons to the revenue officers. The mother gives her youngest son and his girl the chance to get away from the hills to a better life. Emily Fitzroy gave a vivid performance as the browbeaten hillbilly mother. Charles Emmett Mack was outstanding as Tom Tolliver and Elinor Fair, as Essie Hardin, was remarkably forceful, sensitive and natural in her performance. When Brabin tried to distribute the film he was turned down. He was told that audiences wouldn't be interested and it would be a flop.

The National Committee for Better Films was established in 1923. Its paying members received subscriptions to three Board publications, one of which was *Exceptional Photoplays*. In 1923, screenings of the photoplays was held at New York's Town Hall. Brabin's *Driven*, Thomas H. Ince's *Anna Christie* and Robert Boudrioz's *Tillers of the Soil* were viewed. When *Driven* was called a masterpiece, Universal Pictures distributed the six-reel film. It was called one of the best pictures of the year. Brabin signed a long-term contract with Goldwyn.

Later that year, Brabin directed Corinne Griffith and Frank Mayo in *Six Days*, adapted from Elinor Glyn's novel. It was released on September 9, 1923. The story opens aboard an ocean liner bound for England and France. Romance blossoms as the two characters, with the help of a priest as their tour guide, visit battlefields. They become trapped in a German prison trench and for six days they try to dig their way out. The film broke theater attendance records.

It was announced in the *Los Angeles Times* on September 20, 1923, that Brabin, the director of *Six Days* and *Driven*, would direct *Ben-Hur*, to be filmed in Italy. Brabin had been Samuel Goldwyn's favorite choice for the directorial post. The screen version was to be written by June Mathis, one of the highest paid Hollywood executives at that time. Mathis regarded Brabin's film technique to be perfect.

Brabin left the next day for the studio in Rome, accompanied by Theda and Lori, a language interpreter. At the studio Brabin met the cameraman, Silvano Balboni from Genoa. They laid out a plan to film various locations for background footage according to the script for the movie. They filmed footage of the same scenic area at sunrise, noon and in the moonlight. At this time, Benito Mussolini, the leader of the fascist movement, took power. Shooting on location required the permission of the Italian government. The approvals were delayed.

On December 21, 1923, in front of a large crowd, Samuel Goldwyn announced that George Walsh, brother of acclaimed film director Raoul Walsh, would play Ben-Hur and Francis X. Bushman would play Messala. Kathleen Key was selected to play Tizrah. *Ben-Hur* was to be the largest film production in history.

As a screenwriter, Mathis was the first to include details such as stage directions and physical settings in her work. She was known to involve herself with cast, crew, writing and production. Two famous June Mathis sayings are: "I first notice the eyes. There I find what I call soul, and by this alone, I judge." And "If you are vibrating on the right plane, you will inevitably come in contact with the others who can help you. It's like turning on your radio. If you get the right wavelength, you have your station."

In January of 1924, Mathis arrived at the film studio in Rome with the film cuts in her head. The script was to require hundreds of cuts. At their first meeting at the studio, Brabin and Mathis were enthusiastic. Mathis was impressed with Brabin's filming technique, especially the double exposure used in *La Belle Russe* and a closeup scene of the brothers fighting in *Driven*.

Mathis thought that Brabin should direct the closeup scenes and allow the sub-directors to film the crowd scenes. Brabin described some of the perils encountered in filming scenes where hundreds of people would be used and also battle scenes where many things could go wrong. He cited *Cleopatra* as an example of this, and Mathis quickly changed her mind.

Mathis had a romantic interest in George Walsh when he was cast as Ben-Hur. (Walsh was later replaced by Ramon Novarro at the same time Brabin was replaced by Fred Niblo as director.) In March when Walsh arrived, Mathis was being romanced by cameraman Balboni. Walsh had fallen out of favor.

Seventy replica Roman galley ships specially sized for filming were ordered. Mussolini was irate that Goldwyn was paying the Italian workers less money than the American workers. After weeks of strike delays brought on by Mussolini, only thirty vessels were finally delivered to the shore. The long-delayed Italian extras were a mix of irate anti-fascists and fascists who battled their political views amongst themselves.

Mathis was known for her histrionics on set. Brabin set a tone that was favorable with Mathis. He requested that script changes be in writing and that he was not to be interrupted on the set except to approve or reject changes to the script. Brabin said, "I like Silvano Balboni's camerawork; he, of course, was not the best but good enough. The problem that I had is, we would film a scene, I'd turn around and Balboni would be gone! I lost the cameraman to Mathis!"

Theda and Charles resided in a hotel. Theda rarely ventured out of the hotel during the entire stay in Italy. She was uncomfortable going out alone; she felt it was unsafe for her to walk by herself on the streets. She appeared on the *Ben-Hur* set no more than twice.

A day finally arrived after labor strikes and religious holidays when all the crew grouped together on the shores of Anzio. On the day of the filming when the vessels were launched at the shore, the replica galley ships were not seaworthy. Some vessels sank upon launching while others sank in the sea. The extras had to swim ashore; many did not know how to swim. It was feared that some extras had drowned but they were later located further down the beach. All who had participated did survive but it was a terrible experience.

Work was held in abeyance again with labor strikes and reconstruction of the vessels. The reconstructed vessels proved to be more unreliable than the first! The Anzio port authorities allowed the vessels out to sea as long as they remained anchored. This made it very difficult to film a sea battle without the galley ships moving in the sea. To complicate matters even more, when the Italian government learned that the costumes were made in Berlin, they were outraged that the costumes weren't made in Italy. The costumes were pilfered and Brabin resorted to enjoying the Italian wine! Brabin had worked months, sometimes to near-exhaustion, trying to overcome the obstacles.

In April 1924, Goldwyn Pictures merged with Metro Pictures and acquired Louis B. Mayer Pictures, headquartered in Culver City, California. Samuel Goldwyn was forced out. Louis B. Mayer thought that *Ben-Hur* was an out-of-control situation but could be remedied. In July, he replaced Brabin with director Fred Niblo, George Walsh was replaced with Ramon Novarro and June Mathis was fired.

Brabin maintained respect for Mathis. He always stated that she was talented and creative. Brabin said, "The journalists blew up stories but we really didn't have any discord." Mathis made unjust comments, stating that Brabin shot reels of useless footage and had refused her suggestions.

Brabin felt that MGM handled the changes in a dubious way. He feared this outcome would end his career and that his reputation would be ruined by the publicity. Brabin filed suit with his documented proofs of work ordered and Mathis' authorized signature of approval and satisfactions. MGM settled the lawsuit with payment of Brabin's full contract fee and damages.

Mathis had not anticipated the difficulties of strikes, holidays and delays of approvals from the Italian government which escalated the costs and prevented sets from being built. She returned to Hollywood and Silvano Balboni followed. They soon were married.

When Niblo took over, Francis X. Bushman and Kathleen Key were retained. Lori Bara stayed as an interpreter. She received a letter from MGM commending her.

By April 1925, MGM had spent a couple of million dollars in Italy trying to complete *Ben-Hur*. Under Niblo as director, a stunt man was killed when a wheel fell off a chariot during the chariot race at the Roman racetrack. MGM considered firing Niblo; however, they finally realized that the picture could only be finished in Hollywood.

All that remained from the first production of Brabin's *Ben-Hur* was a cabinet full of black-and-white still photographs and some film footage. The photographs showed the actors with wigs sliding off their heads in a mishmash of costumes that didn't fit, desert scenes and camels, anchored galley ships and sinking vessels. When Theda and Charles returned home to Hollywood, thousands of letters poured in requesting Theda to return to the screen.

Brabin went into production on Edna Ferber's *So Big* starring Colleen Moore and Wallace Beery. In *So Big* Moore's character aged over three decades; she gave one of her best dramatic performances. The film was released on December 28, 1924, by First National Pictures and was a box office success. (Brabin again directed Moore in *Twinkletoes*, a light comedy that tells the story of a Cockney waif of the London Limehouse district who aspires to be a dancer. It was a smash hit in 1926.)

In 1925, Brabin directed a remake of Mary Pickford's 1918 film *Stella Maris*. Mary Philbin played Stella Maris and Unity Blake, two different characters. Brabin captured "both" Philbins using a split screen and double exposures. Elliott Dexter, Gladys Brockwell and Jason Robards, Sr., gave noteworthy supporting performances. *Stella Maris* was released by Universal on December 13, 1925.

Shortly after the release of *Stella Maris*, Theda received the shocking news of the death of J. Gordon Edwards, director general of Fox Film Corporation. He became sick with a cold on Christmas Day but refused to stay out of the cold weather. He died of pneumonia in his residence at the Hotel Plaza in New York City on December 31, 1925.

Brabin's *Mismates* (1926) was based on Myron C. Fagan's stage play. It starred Doris Kenyon and Warner Baxter and featured lavish scenes of the most beautiful girls in New York City, dancing girls riding on chariots drawn by Nubian slaves and a jewelry parade scene with models displaying priceless jewelry. The box office success was released by First National Pictures on July 26, 1926.

Brabin directed *Framed* on location in the diamond mines of Brazil. The film was an adaptation of the story "The Dawn of My Tomorrow" by George W. Sutton, Jr. It featured Milton Sills and Natalie Kingston and was released by First National Pictures. It was the story of people trapped in the diamond mines of Brazil when an avalanche of mud turns into a sea of death.

Brabin's *Hard-Boiled Haggerty* starring Milton Sills and Molly O'Day was a rapid fire aerial World War I thriller with comedic elements thrown in. The film was replete with many dogfights. Sol Polito, known for his craftsmanship and crisp images, was hired as cinematographer. After the merger of First National Studios and Warner Brothers in 1928, Polito became chief cinematographer with Tony Gaudio at Warner Brothers. Walter Plunkett is credited in this film with his first job assignment as a costume designer. His career extended to 156 films. He became the most famous costume designer for film, Broadway shows and the Metropolitan Opera. He is remembered for *Gone with the Wind* (particularly the green velvet dress worn by Scarlett O'Hara) and his Oscar win for costume design in *An American in Paris*.

Brabin directed *The Valley of the Giants* starring Milton Sills and his wife Doris Kenyon. Filmed in some of the locations of the story and in Yosemite by cinematographer Ted McCord, the film tells the heart-rending story of the wife of a timber baron trying to save her favorite part of the redwood forest from destruction by the lumber industry.

During the filming of *The Valley of the Giants*, while Theda was with Charles in Sequoia Park, she was told about a theater named the Imperial in Humboldt County. In 1916, the owner of the theater ran an essay contest. A ten dollar gold piece was offered as the prize for the best entry titled, "Why I would like Theda Bara for a wife."

Shortly afterward, Brabin directed Louis Stevens' adaptation of Jack London's novel *Burning Daylight*, the story of a tycoon who makes a million dollars in the Klondike gold strike and loses it in San Francisco. It starred Milton Sills and Doris Kenyon. In Brabin's next project, Vitaphone's *The Whip*, he cast his old friend Marc McDermott, Dorothy Mackaill, Ralph Forbes and Anna Q. Nilsson. In the story, a British nobleman loses his memory in an accident and in his amnesiac condition he becomes the trainer of a horse named The Whip, which is slated to run at Ascot. *The Whip* was McDermott's last film. He became ill during the filming and died on January 5, 1929. Milton Sills died after playing tennis with his wife Doris Kenyon in 1930. It was noted in his obituary that *Burning Daylight* and *The Valley of the Giants* were amongst the best of his motion pictures.

In 1929, Brabin directed the film version of Thornton Wilder's Pulitzer Prize–winning story *The Bridge of San Luis Rey* starring the famed silent screen villain, Ernest Torrence. Lili Damita, a French actress, was hired because her speaking voice could be recorded well. Don Alvarado played the role as Manuel. A friar played by Henry B. Walthall tells of the lives of interrelated people who die in the collapse of an Inca rope-fiber suspension bridge in Peru, and the events that led to their being on the bridge. The film was released in 1929 by MGM in both silent and part-talkie versions. Cedric Gibbons was awarded the second Academy Award for Best Art Director. Gibbons is also known for designing the Oscar statuette.

Brabin's *The Ship from Shanghai* was the first all-talking film that was made almost entirely at sea. It was released by MGM on January 1, 1930. The screenplay by John Howard Lawson was adapted from Dale Collins' novel, *Ordeal*. The movie tells the story of a yachting party of rich socialites sailing from Shanghai. Conrad Nagel, Kay Johnson and Carmel Myers endure a terrific storm. The passengers fall into the hands of a crazy steward (Louis Wolheim) who takes control of the water supply. It was filmed off of Catalina Island in California.

John Howard Lawson, a Marxist, adamantly opposed the House Committee on Un-American activities and was blacklisted in the late 1940s. The heart, mind and soul of the communist community in Hollywood, he was a founder and first president of the Writers Guild of America.

Brabin directed the musical *Call of the Flesh* with Ramon Novarro, in his first talking picture. Writers John Colton and Dorothy Farnum delivered a charming, heartwarming story with beautiful music. Co-star Renee Adoree became ill on the set and doctors ordered her to quit at once. Renee pleaded for a half-hour to keep working and delivered her finest performance.

In 1931 Brabin directed *The Great Meadow* which he co-authored with Elizabeth M. Roberts. A historical drama set in 1777, the story depicted the hardships of a courageous band of settlers traveling to Daniel Boone's "Gateway to Kaintuck" to find the Promised Land in a "great meadow" (now central Kentucky). Characters played by Johnny Mack Brown and Eleanor Boardman were intended to resemble the author's own pioneer ancestors.

Brabin's next film *Sporting Blood*, a thrilling true-life story, starred Ernest Torrence as a horse trainer, Clark Gable in his first starring role as gambler "Rid" Riddell, and Madge Evans as Miss Ruby, the owner of a horse named Tommy Boy. The film focused on the love of horses and did so specifically for the first 30 minutes without the presence of any of the stars. It then took the audience into the excitement of horse racing. *Sporting Blood* was filmed in Hopkinsville, Kentucky, and released by MGM in August of 1931. It was produced by Marion Davies.

Brabin's *The Beast of the City* (1932) opened with President Herbert Hoover's plea to stop glamorizing gangsters. Walter Huston and

12. Charles Brabin

Jean Harlow made the screen sizzle. Theda Bara prepared Jean Harlow for the lineup scene that is so well remembered. Huston played the fighting police captain pitted against politicians. Wallace Ford played the brother of a police captain who falls for Daisy (Harlow), a double-crossing blonde who led men to kill. Jean Hersholt played the bootleg boss Sam Belmonte. *The Beast of the City* ranks as one of the top shoot-out films.

Executive Paul Bern had arranged for MGM to borrow Harlow for the film. On Harlow's twenty-first birthday in 1932, Bern told Harlow that her contract with Howard Hughes had been bought out by MGM. Bern married Harlow in June, and two months later Bern was declared dead by suicide.

Brabin's next film, *New Morals for Old*, was adapted from John Van Druten's play *After All*. It starred Robert Young in his first leading role, with Margaret Perry in her first screen appearance. Lewis Stone, Laura Hope Crews, Ruth Selwyn, Myrna Loy, and Jean Hersholt rounded out the cast. The plot involved rebellious children and their parents who have lost sight of themselves. Young became known as the greatest dad in the television series *Father Knows Best* during the 1950s and as Dr. Marcus Welby in the *Marcus Welby, M.D.* series in the 1960s.

The Washington Masquerade, Brabin's next film, was adapted from Henri Bernstein's play, *The Claw*. Lionel Barrymore plays a Senator who becomes a national power and leader in the fight for public ownership of utilities. The dramatic climax occurs in the Senate chambers where Barrymore's speech exposes the structure of "inside" politics. Hattie McDaniel made herself known as an actress in this film. She later won an Oscar for Best Supporting Actress in *Gone with the Wind*.

Brabin last film of 1931 was *The Mask of Fu Manchu*, starring Boris Karloff as the man-monster and Myrna Loy as Karloff's dragon lady daughter. Lewis Stone is an English official searching the hidden tomb of Genghis Khan. Dr. Fu Manchu seeks to seize a buried talisman, proclaiming himself the reincarnation of Genghis Khan, with the intent to start an Asiatic uprising against Europe. The film had Oriental intrigue, strange crimes, weird underground torture cells, and the amazing laboratory of the "death ray." One scene included a gold-plated Buddha 50 feet high. The supporting stars were Jean Hersholt, Karen Morley, and Charles Starrett. The film opened in Hollywood at the Pantages Theater.

Brabin directed *The Secret of Madame Blanche* (1933), adapted from Martin Brown's play *The Lady* by Frances Goodrich and Albert Hackett. The cast included Irene Dunne, Lionel Atwill, Phillips Holmes, Una Merkel and Douglas Walton. In this World War I melodrama, Madame Blanche has a secret similar to that of Madame X. *The Secret of Madame Blanche* was released by MGM in February of 1933.

MGM announced plans to film *Rasputin and the Empress,* a prestigious picture without budget or time limitations. Lionel, John, and Ethel Barrymore had been secured as stars and Brabin was chosen to direct. The Barrymore siblings had never appeared together in a sound motion picture. The first draft included a number of troubling scenes, one portraying a scandalous incident suggesting that the princess had given herself to Rasputin, which never actually happened. It was also problematic that some of the characters in this historical drama were based on people who were still alive.

During the filming, there were so many script re-writes and revisions that it resulted in confusion and frustration by all. The Barrymores were accustomed to being catered to, particularly Ethel. The siblings argued continually amongst themselves and Ethel clashed with Brabin. She refused to take direction and paid no attention to blocking. Scene after scene had to be re-shot. Ethel mocked Brabin in front of everyone on the set and called him "Mr. Theda Bara." Brabin said he walked out. Producer Irving Thalberg replaced him with Richard Boleslawski.

Ethel continued to be extraordinarily difficult. It proved to be a financial disaster for MGM. A libel lawsuit was filed by Prince Felix Yusupov and the Russian Princess Irena, the still living principals of the historic Rasputin tale.

The scenes that Brabin filmed remained in the film but all the credit went to Boleslawski. Amazingly, *Rasputin and the Empress* was nominated for Best Original Screenplay at the 1933 Academy Awards. Prince Yusupov and Princess Irena were awarded substantial damages for defamation of character against Thalberg and MGM.

Brabin next directed MGM's *Stage Mother* starring Alice Brady, Maureen O'Sullivan, Franchot Tone, Ted Healy and Phillips Holmes, a musical melodrama about a stage mother and her daughter. O'Sullivan, as the daughter, sings "I'm Dancing on a Rainbow." Alice Brady sings "Any Little Girl," "Thar's a Nice Girl," and "Is the Right Little Girl for Me." The film was released in September 1933.

Day of Reckoning, Brabin's next project, was adapted from Morris

Lavine's novel by Zelda Sears. It starred Richard Dix, Madge Evans, Conway Teale, Una Merkel, Stuart Erwin, and George "Spanky" McFarland. It was an enjoyable tale of love and vengeance in a jailhouse. *Day of Reckoning* was filmed with special effects including a breathtaking fight on top of a tall building in downtown Los Angeles. The film was released by MGM in October 1933.

A Wicked Woman, Brabin's last film, was adapted by Zelda Sears from Anne Austin's novel of the same name. It starred Mady Christians, Jean Parker, Charles Bickford, Betty Furness, and William Henry. Sears, a scenarist and screenwriter for Cecil B. DeMille and MGM, also played a part in the film. This was her final film. MGM released *A Wicked Woman* in December 1934. Sears passed away several months later.

Brabin Filmography

1911

The Awakening of John Bond—Edison Company
Bigelow Cooper, Miriam Nesbitt, Mary Fuller, Harold M. Shaw, Philip Tannura, Kathleen Coughlan.

1912

What Happened to Mary—Edison Company
Mary Fuller, Marc McDermott, Charles Ogle, Barry O'Moore, Bliss Milford, Bigelow Cooper, William Wadsworth, Miriam Nesbitt, Harold M. Shaw.
The Usurer's Grip—Edison Company
Walter Edwin, Gertrude McCoy, Edna May Weick, Charles Ogle, Louise Sydmeth, Robert Brower.
Under False Colors—Edison Company
Augustus Phillips, Gertrude McCoy, Robert Brower, Louise Sydmeth, George Lessey.
A Soldier's Duty—Edison Company
Augustus Phillips, Gertrude McCoy, George Lessey, Wadsworth Harris, Harry Linson.
The Affair at Raynor's—Edison Company
Mary Fuller, William Wadsworth, William Bechtel, Alice Washburn, Edna Hammel, Walter Edwin, Robert Brower, Marc McDermott, Charles Ogle, Barry O'Moore, Harry M. Shaw, May Abbey.

Young Mrs. Eaton—Edison Company
   Gertrude McCoy, Augustus Phillips, Louise Beaudet, Robert Brower.
A Baby's Shoe—Edison Company
   Walter Edwin, Robert Brower, Gertrude McCoy, Helen Coughlin.
The Non-Commissioned Officer—Edison Company
   Walter Edwin, Charles Ogle, Robert Brower, Gertrude McCoy, Augustus Phillips.
Hope, a Red Cross Seal Story—Edison Company
   George Lessey, Gertrude McCoy, William West, Robert Brower, Charles Ogle.
Tim—Edison Company
   Charles Ogle, Barry O'Moore, Robert Brower, Mrs. William Bechtel.
A Dollar Saved Is a Dollar Earned—Edison Company
   Augustus Phillips, Bliss Milford, George Lessey.
His Mother's Hope—Edison Company
   George Lessey, Gertrude McCoy, Barry O'Moore, Bessie Learn, Louise Sydmeth, Martin Fuller, William Porter, Jr.
Annie Crawls Upstairs—Edison Company
   Robert Brower, Ida Williams, Helen Coughlin, Edna Flugrath, Margery Bonney Erskine, Bigelow Cooper, Mrs. William Bechtel, Gertrude McCoy, Harry Beaumont, Elizabeth Miller, Edna Hammel, Barry O'Moore.

1913

An Unsullied Shield—Edison Company
   Wadsworth Harris, Marc McDermott, Margery Bonney Erskine, Mabel Trunnell, Bessie Learn, Harry Eytinge, Herbert Pryor, Walter Edwin, Agustus Phillips.
The Maid of Honor—Edison Company
   Marc McDermott, Mabel Trunnelle, Bessie Learn, Margery Erskine.
Leonie—Edison Company
   Augustus Phillips, Mary Fuller, Miriam Nesbitt, Margery Bonney Erskine, Mrs. William Bechtel, Harry Beaumont, George Lessey, Walter Edwin.
The Mountaineers—Edison Company
   Charles Ogle, Gertrude McCoy, Augustus Phillips, William West, Walter Edwin, George Lessey.
The Ambassador's Daughter—Edison Company
   Miriam Nesbitt, George Lessey, Robert Brower, Marc McDermott, Charles Ogle, Mary Fuller.
The Princess and the Man—Edison Company
   Marc McDermott, Mary Fuller, Charles Ogle, Miriam Nesbitt, Augustus Phillips, Richard Ridgely, Bigelow Cooper, Robert Brower.

His Enemy—Edison Company
   Herbert Yost, Mrs. Bechtel, Richard Ridgely, Gertrude McCoy, William West, Augustus Phillips.
The Minister's Temptation—Edison Company
   Augustus Phillips, Mary Fuller, Robert Brower, Marc McDermott.
A Will and a Way—Edison Company
   Mary Fuller, William Wadsworth, Richard Ridgely, Mrs. Bechtel, William West, Bigelow Cooper.
Kathleen Mavourneen—Edison Company
   Mary Fuller, Marc McDermott, Augustus Phillips, William West, Gertrude McCoy, Harry Linson, Harry Gripp.
The Risen Soul of Jim Grant—Edison Company
   Harry Gripp, Cora Williams, Shirley Mason, Herbert Prior, Margery Erskine, Augustus Phillips, Richard Ridgely, Ida Williams.
A Concerto for the Violin—Edison Company
   Marc McDermott, Miriam Nesbitt, Mabel Trunnelle.
Mercy Merrick—Edison Company
   Mary Fuller, Robert Brower, Bigelow Cooper, Gertrude McCoy, Margery Bonney Erskine, Richard Tucker.
While John Bolt Slept—Edison Company
   Marc McDermott, Charles Ogle, Robert Brower, Richard Ridgely, Augustus Phillips, Miriam Nesbitt, Nellie Grant.
The Coast Guard's Sister—Edison Company
   Winifred Albion, Frederick Annerley, Warren Foster, James LaFre, Marc McDermott, Miriam Nesbitt, Edwin Perin.
Flood Tide—Edison Company
   Frederick Annerley, Alice Mansfield, Marc McDermott, Fanny Midgley, Miriam Nesbitt.
Keepers of the Flock—Edison Company
   John Le Fre, Marc McDermott, Miriam Nesbitt, Carles Vernon.
Cornwall, the English Riviera—Edison Company
The Stroke of the Phoebus Eight—Edison Company
   Marc McDermott, Miriam Nesbitt, Charles Vernon.
A Daughter of Romany—Edison Company
   William Albion, Marc McDermott, Miriam Nesbitt.
The Foreman's Treachery—Edison Company
   Marc McDermott, Miriam Nesbitt, Charles Vernon, Douglas Munro.
Silas Marner—Edison Company
   Yale Benner, Robert Brower, Bigelow Cooper, Gladys Hulette, William West, C.J. Williams.
The Stolen Plans—Edison Company

Marc McDermott, Miriam Nesbitt, Charles Vernon, William Luff, Winifred Albion.
A Race to New York—Edison Company
Mary Fuller, Charles Ogle, Barry O'Moore, Augustus Phillips, Edna Flugrath, Herbert Prior.

1914

The Antique Brooch—Edison Company
Marc McDermott, Miriam Nesbitt, Kathleen Russell.
The Necklace of Ramses—Edison Company
Mrs. W. Bechtel, William Bechtel, Gertrude Braun, Robert Brower, Marjorie Ellison, Mary Fuller, Rex Ingram, Marc McDermott, Miriam Nesbitt, Charles Vernon.
All for His Sake—Edison Company
William Brechtel, Augustus Carney, Gertrude McCoy, Marc McDermott, Ben F. Wilson
The Price of the Necklace—Edison Company
Rex Ingram, Charles Ogle.
The Man Who Disappeared—Edison Company
Marc McDermott, Herbert Yost, Miriam Nesbitt, Marjorie Ellison, Cora Williams, Harry Eytinge, Charles Ogle, T. Tamamoto, Harry Mason, Harry Linson, Joseph Manning, Floyd France, George D. Melville, Warren Cook.
The Black Mask—Edison Company
Marc McDermott, Barry O'Moore, Miriam Nesbitt.
A Hunted Animal—Edison Company
Marc McDermott, Barry O'Moore, Miriam Nesbitt, Duncan McRae, T. Tamamoto, Harry Mason.
The Double Cross—Edison Company
Marc McDermott, Barry O'Moore, Miriam Nesbitt, Charles Ogle, Harry Eytinge, Cora Williams, T. Tamamoto.
The Light on the Wall—Edison Company
Marc McDermott, Barry O'Moore, Miriam Nesbitt, Charles Ogle, Harry Eytinge, Marjorie Ellison, Margaret McWade, Horace Newman.
With His Hands—Edison Company
Marc McDermott, Barry O'Moore, Miriam Nesbitt, Marjorie Ellison, Harry Linson, Joseph Manning, Floyd France, George D. Melville, Warren Cook.
The Gap—Edison Company
Marc McDermott, Barry O'Moore, Miriam Nesbitt, Marjorie Ellison, Harry Linson, Joseph Manning, Horace Newman.

The Man in the Street—Edison Company
  Gertrude McCoy, Marc McDermott, Charles Ogle, Duncan McRay.
Face to Face—Edison Company
  Marc McDermott, Barry O'Moore, Miriam Nesbitt, Marjorie Ellison, Harry Linson, Joseph Manning, Horace Newman.
A Matter of Minutes—Edison Company
  Marc McDermott, Barry O'Moore, Miriam Nesbitt.
The Living Dead—Edison Company
  Marc McDermott, Barry O'Moore, Miriam Nesbitt, Harry Mason.
The President's Special—Edison Company
  Charles Ogle, Gertrude McCoy, George W. Anson, Margaret McWade, Shirley Mason, Robert Brower.
By the Aid of a Film—Edison Company
  Marc McDermott, Barry O'Moore, Miriam Nesbitt, Harry Mason, W.A. Whitecar, John H. Collins.
The Long Way—Edison Company
  Robert Brower, Robert Conness, Marc McDermott, Duncan McRae, Miriam Nesbitt, Mabel Trunnelle.
The Letter That Never Came Out—Edison Company
  Sally Crute, Herbert Prior.
The Midnight Ride of Paul Revere—Edison Company
  Augustus Phillips, Carlton S. King, Harry Linson, Yale Benner, Richard Tucker, Saul Harrison.
A Question of Identity—Edison Company
  Julia Calhoun, Augustus Phillips, Carlton S. King, Warren Cook, Bessie Learn, Mabel Trunnelle, Edward Earle, Mrs. William Bechtel, William West.
The King's Move on the City—Edison Company
  Marc McDermott, Miriam Nesbitt.
The Best Man—Edison Company
  Marc McDermott, Gertrude McCoy, Mrs. W. Bechtel, Pat O'Malley, Robert Brower, Duncan McRae.
The Birth of Our Savior—Edison Company
  Harry Eytinge, Carlton S. King, Harry Linson, Gertrude McCoy, Frank McGlynn Sr., Charles Sutton.
The Premature Comprise—Edison Company
  Marc McDermott, Duncan McRae.

1915

An Invitation and an Attack—Edison Company
  Yale Benner, Marc McDermott, Duncan McRae.

Her Husband's Son—Edison Company
Robert Conness, Gertrude McCoy, Harry Beaumont, Helen Strickland, Jessie Stevens.
A Theft in the Dark—Edison Company
Marc McDermott, Miriam Nesbitt, Viola Dana, Edward Earle, Harry Linson, Yale Benner.
The Stoning—Edison Company
Viola Dana, Robert Conness, Helen Strickland, Charles Sutton, Yale Boss, Harry Beaumont, Ruth Clifford.
The House of the Lost Court—Edison Company
Robert Conness, Duncan McRae, Helen Strickland, Sally Crute, Viola Dana, Margery Erskine, Gertrude McCoy, William West.
The Woman Hater—Edison Company
Charles Brabin, Edna Mayo, Henry B. Walthall, Bryant Washburn.
Vanity Fair—Edison Company
Minnie Maddern Fiske, Shirley Mason, Helen Fulton, William Wadsworth, Richard Tucker, Robert Brower, Frank McGlynn Sr., Bigelow Cooper, George A. Wright, Maurice Steuart, Ellen Strickland, Philip Quinn, John Sturgeon, Arthur Row.
The Raven—Essanay Film Company
Henry B. Walthall, Warda Howard, Ernest Maupain, Eleanor Thompson, Marian Skinner, Harry Dunkinson, Grant Foreman, Hugh Thompson, Peggy Meredith, Frank Hamilton, Billy Robinson, Bert Weston.

1916

The Bridesmaid's Secret—Essanay Film Company
John Lorenz, Marian Murray, Fritzi Ridgeway.
That Sort—Essanay Film Company
Betty Brown, Warda Howard, John Lorenz, Ernst Maupain, Duncan McRae, Marian Skinner, Peggy Sweeney.
The Higher Destiny—Essanay Film Company
Warda Howard, Sidney Ainsworth, Edward Arnold, Gertrude Glover, Patrick Calhoun.
The Price of Fame—Vitagraph Company of America
Marc McDermott, Naomi Childers, L. Rogers Lyton, Logan Paul, Mary Maurice, Philip Quinn.
The Secret Kingdom—Vitagraph Company of America
Charles Richman, Dorothy Kelly, Joseph Kilgour, Arline Pretty, William R. Dunn, De Jalma West, Ned Finley, Charles Wellesley, Robert Whitworth.

1917

Babette—Vitagraph Company of America
   Marc McDermott, Peggy Hyland, Templar Saxe, William R. Dunn.
The Sixteenth Wife—Vitagraph Company of America
   Peggy Hyland, Marc McDermott, George J. Forth, Templar Saxe.
Mary Jane's Pa—Vitagraph Company of America
   Marc McDermott, Mindred Manng, Eulalie Jensen, Emmett King, Clio Ayres, William R. Dunn, Templar Saxe, Edward Elkas, Mary Maurice, Billy Bletcher, Maxine Elliott Hicks.
The Adopted Son—Rolfe Photoplays
   Francis X. Bushman, Beverly Bayne, Leslie Stowe, Jack W. Johnston, John Smiley, Gertrude Norman, Pat O'Malley.
Persuasive Peggy—Mayfair Film Corporation
   Peggy Hyland, William B. Davidson, Mary Cecil, Gertrude Norman, Charles Sutton, Jules Cowles, Arthur Housman.
Red, White and Blue Blood—Metro Pictures Corporation
   Francis X. Bushman, Beverly Bayne, Adella Barker, William H. Tooker, Duncan McRae, Cecil Fletcher, John Raymond, C.R. McKinney, Arthur Housman.

1918

Breakers Ahead—Metro Picture Corporation
   Viola Dana, Clifford Bruce, Mabel Van Buren, Russell Simpson, Eugene Pallette, Sydney Deane, Gibson Gowland, Lorena Foster, Helen Jerome Eddy.
Social Quicksands—Metro Picture Corporation
   Francis X. Bushman, Beverly Bayne, Mabel Frenyear, Leslie Stowe, William R. Dunn, Leila Blow, Rolinda Bainbridge, Elsie MacLeod, Jack B. Hollis, Armorel McDowell, William Stone, Jack Dunn.
A Pair of Cupids—Metro Picture Corporation
   Francis X. Bushman, Beverly Bayne, Charles Sutton, Gerald Griffin, Jessie Stevens, Edgar Norton, Lou Gorey, Mrs. Turner, Tom Blake, Louis Wolheim, John Judge, Elwell Judge.
His Bonded Wife—Metro Picture Corporation
   Emmy Wehlen, Frank Currier, Creighton Hale, Warda Howard, William Frederic.
Buchanan's Wife—Fox Film Corporation
   Virginia Pearson, Marc McDermott, Victor Sutherland, Ned Finley.
The Poor Rich Man—Metro Pictures
   Francis X. Bushman, Beverly Bayne, Stuart Holmes, Sally Crute, William Frederic, C.J. Williams, Jules Cowles, Louis Wolheim.

1919

Thou Shalt Not—Fox Film Corporation
　Evelyn Nesbit, Ned Burton, Florida Kingsley, Gladden James, Crauford Kent, Edmund Lawrence.
Kathleen Mavourneen—Fox Film Corporation
　Theda Bara, Edward O'Connor, Jennie Dickerson, Raymond McKee, Marc McDermott, Marcia Harris, Henry Hallam, Harry Gripp, Morgan Thorpe.
La Belle Russe—Fox Film Corporation
　Theda Bara, Warburton Gamble, Robert Lee Keeling, William B. Davidson, Alice Wilson, Robert Vivian, Lewis Broughton.

1920

While New York Sleeps—Fox Film Corporation
　Estelle Taylor, William Locke, Marc McDermott, Harry Sothern, Earl Metcalfe.
Blind Wives—Fox Film Corporation
　Marc McDermott, Estelle Taylor, Harry Sothern, Annette Bracy, Sally Crute, Robert Schable.

1921

Footfalls—Fox Film Corporation
　Tyrone Power, Sr., Tom Douglas, Estelle Taylor, Gladden James.

1922

The Broadway Peacock—Fox Film Corporation
　Pearl White, Joseph Striker, Doris Eaton, Harry Southard, Elizabeth Garrison.
The Lights of New York—Fox Film Corporation
　Clarence Nordstrom, Margaret Seddon, Frank Currier, Florence Short, Charles K. Gerrard, Marc McDermott, Estelle Taylor.

1923

Driven—Charles J. Brabin Productions
　Emily Fitzroy, Burr McIntosh, Charles Emmett Mack, George Bancroft, Fred Koser, Ernest Chandler, Leslie Stowe, Elinor Fair.
Six Days—Goldwyn Pictures Corporation
　Corinne Griffith, Frank Mayo, Myrtle Stedman, Claude King, Maude

George, Spottiswoode Aitken, Charles Clary, Evelyn Walsh Hall, Paul Cazenueve, Jack Herbert, Robert DeVilbiss.

1924

So Big—First National Pictures
 Colleen Moore, Joseph De Grasse, John Bowers, Ben Lyon, Wallace Beery, Gladys Brockwell, Jean Hersholt, Charlotte Merriam, Dot Farley, Ford Sterling, Frankie Darro, Henry Herbert.

1925

Stella Maris—Universal Pictures
 Mary Philbin, Eliott Dexter, Gladys Brockwell, Jason Robards Sr., Phillips Smalley, Lillian Lawrence, Robert Bolder, Aileen Manning.
Ben-Hur: A Tale of the Christ—Metro-Goldwyn-Mayer (Brabin was uncredited).
 Ramon Novarro, Francis X. Bushman, May McAvoy, Betty Bronson, Claire McDowell, Kathleen Key, Carmel Myers.

1926

Mismates—First National Pictures
 Doris Kenyon, Warner Baxter, May Allison, Philo McCullough, Charles Murray, Maude Turner Gordon, John Kolb, Cyril Ring, Nancy Kelly.
Twinkletoes—John McCormack Productions
 Colleen Moore, Kenneth Harlan, Tully Marshall, Gladys Brockwell, Lucien Littlefield, Warner Oland, John Kolb, Julianne Johnston, William McDonald, Dorothy Vernon, Ned Sparks, Dick Sutherland.

1927

Framed—First National Pictures
 Milton Sills, Natalie Kingston, E.J. Ratcliffe, Charles K. Gerrard, Edward Peil Sr., Burr McIntosh, Natli Barr, John Miljan.
Hard-Boiled Haggerty—First National Pictures
 Milton Sills, Molly O'Day, Mitchell Lewis, Arthur Stone, George Fawcett, Yola d'Avril.
The Valley of the Giants—First National Pictures
 Milton Sills, Doris Kenyon, Arthur Stone, George Fawcett, Paul Hurst, Yola d'Avril, Phil Brady, James A. Marcus, Erville Alderson, Dan Crimmins, Oto Hoffman, Lucien Littlefield, Dan Mason, Charles Sellon.

1928

Burning Daylight—First National Pictures
  Milton Sills, Doris Kenyon, Arthur Stone, Guinn Williams, Lawford Davidson, Jane Winton, Stuart Holmes, Edmund Breese, Howard Truesdale, Frank Hagney, Harry Northrup, George Cowl, Richard Cramer.
The Whip—First National Pictures
  Dorothy Mackaill, Ralph Forbes, Anna Q. Nilsson, Lowell Sherman, Albert Gran, Marc McDermott, Louis Payne, Arthur Clayton.

1929

The Bridge of San Luis Rey—Metro-Goldwyn-Mayer
  Lili Damita, Ernest Torrence, Raquel Torres, Don Alvarado, Duncan Renaldo, Henry B. Walthall, Michael Vavitch, Emily Fitzroy, Jane Winton, Gordon Thorpe, Mitchell Lewis, Paul Ellis, Eugenie Besserer.

1930

The Ship from Shanghai—Metro-Goldwyn-Mayer
  Conrad Nagel, Kay Johnson, Carmel Myers, Holmes Herbert, Zeffie Tilbury, Louis Wolheim, Ivan Linow, Jack McDonald, Henry Armetta, Willie Fung, Pietro Gentile, Pat Harmon, Albert MacQuarrie.
Call of the Flesh—Metro-Goldwyn-Mayer
  Ramon Novarro, Dorothy Jordan, Ernest Torrence, Nance O'Neil, Renee Adoree, Mathilde Comont, Russell Hopton, Julia Griffith, Fred Hueston, Adolph Milar, Leo White, Frank Yaconelli.

1931

The Great Meadow—Metro-Goldwyn-Mayer
  Johnny Mack Brown, Eleanor Boardman, Lucille La Verne, Anita Louise, Gavin Gordon, Guinn Williams, Russell Simpson, Sarah Padden, Helen Jerome Eddy, Julie Haydon, William Bakewell, James Bradbury Jr.
Sporting Blood—Metro-Goldwyn-Mayer
  Clark Gable, Ernest Torrence, Madge Evans, Lew Cody, Marie Prevost, Hallam Cooley, J. Farrell MacDonald, John Larkin, Eugene Hackson, Tommy Boy, Sidney Bracey.

1932

The Beast of the City—Metro-Goldwyn-Mayer
  Walter Huston, Jean Harlow, Wallace Ford, Jean Hersholt, Dorothy Peterson, Tully Marshall, John Miljan, Emmett Corrigan, Warner Rich-

mond, Sandy Roth, J. Carrol Naish, Eddie Baker, Elmer Ballard, Sammy Blum.

New Morals for Old—Metro-Goldwyn-Mayer
Robert Young, Margaret Perry, Lewis Stone, Laura Hope Crews, Myrna Loy, David Newell, Jean Hersholt, Ruth Selwyn, Kathryn Crawford, Louise Closser Hale, Mitchell Lewis, Elizabeth Patterson, Lillian Harmer.

The Washington Masquerade—Metro-Goldwyn-Mayer
Lionel Barrymore, Karen Morley, Diane Sinclair, Nils Asther, Reginald Barlow, William Collier, Sr., William Morris, Rafaela Ottiano, C. Henry Gordon, Berton Churchill, Henry Kolker, Oscar Apfel, Sidney Bracey.

The Mask of Fu Manchu—Metro-Goldwyn-Mayer
Boris Karloff, Lewis Stone, Karen Morley, Myrna Loy, Jean Hersholt, Lawrence Grant, David Torrence, Herbert Bunston, Gertrude Michael, Everett Brown, Steve Clemente, Willie Fung, Ferdinand Gottschalk.

Rasputin and the Empress—Metro-Goldwyn-Mayer (Brabin was uncredited).
John Barrymore, Ethel Barrymore, Lionel Barrymore, Ralph Morgan, Tad Alexander, Diana Wynyard, C. Henry Gordon, Edward Arnold, Clarence Wilson, Luis Alberni, Mary Alden, Robert Anderson, Oscar Apfel.

1933

The Secret of Madame Blanche—Metro-Goldwyn-Mayer
Irene Dunne, Lionel Atwill, Phillips Holmes, Una Merkel, Douglas Walton, C. Henry Gordon, Jean Parker, Mitchell Lewis, William Bakewell, Robert Adair, Norman Ainsley, Albert Conti, Edward Cooper.

Stage Mother—Metro-Goldwyn-Mayer
Alice Brady, Maureen O'Sullivan, Franchot Tone, Phillips Holmes, Ted Healy, Russell Hardie, C. Henry Gordon, Alan Edwards, Ben Alexander, Lowden Adams, Luis Alberni, Sam Ash, Hank Bell, Margaret Bert.

Day of Reckoning—Metro-Goldwyn-Mayer
Richard Dix, Madge Evans, Conway Tearle, Una Merkel, Stuart Erwin, George McFarland, Isabel Jewell, James Bell, Raymond Hatton, Paul Hurst, John Larkin, Wilfred Lucas, Samuel S. Hinds, Ernie Adams.

1934

A Wicked Woman—Metro-Goldwyn-Mayer
Mady Christians, Jean Parker, Charles Bickford, Betty Furness, William Henry, Jackie Searl, Betty Jane Graham, Marilyn Harris, Paul Harvey, Zelda Sears, Robert Taylor, Sterling Holloway, Georgie Billings.

Writer's Credits

A Soldier's Duty (1912), *An Unsullied Shield* (1913), *Kathleen Mavourneen* (1913), *Mercy Merrick* (1913), *Dolly Varden* (1913), *The Pied Piper of Hamelin* (1913), *Silas Marner* (1913), *The Stoning* (1915), *The Raven* (1915), *That Sort* (1916), *The Price of Fame* (1916), *Persuasive Peggy* (1917), *Breakers Ahead* (1918), *Thou Shalt Not* (1919), *Kathleen Mavourneen* (1919), *La Belle Russe* (1919), *While New York Sleeps* (1920), *Blind Wives* (1920), *Footfalls* (1921), *The Lights of New York* (1922), *Stella Maris* (1925), *The Great Meadow* (1931), *Sporting Blood* (1931).

Index

Numbers in **bold italics** indicate pages with photographs.

Abbey Church of St. Peter, Westminster 89
Academy Awards 75, 186
Academy of Motion Picture Arts and Sciences 65
Adams-Mastrovich Family Foundation 98; see also Balmat, Mary Adams (donor)
Adamson, Harold 38, 69
After All 187
Aladdin's Lamp 42
Algerian Desert 134
All Saints Episcopal Church, Beverly Hills, CA 80
Alvarado, Don 185
Ambassador to Luxembourg 87
American Beauties 10
An American in Paris 185
American Indian 17
American Products Company 16
American Theater Wing 62
An American Tragedy 80
Anaheim, California 98
Andersen, Hans Christian 65
Anderson, Gilbert M. 179
Anderson, Maxwell 55–56, 62–64, 66
Animal Sanctuary, Nova Scotia 179
Anna Christie 180
Annie Get Your Gun 88
Anspacher, Louis K 168
Any Little Girl 188
Anzio, Italy 182
April Showers 82
The Archangel of Destiny 125
Asheville, North Carolina 126
Astaire, Ava 26, 49, 76–*77*, 78
Astaire, Lady Charles Cavendish 96
Astaire, Fred 96
Atwill, Lionel 188
Audley, Lady 121
August, Edwin 178
Austin, Anne 189
Avondale, Ohio 5, 8

Avril, Nancy 178
Azure Baths of Cordova 123

Balboa Island, Newport Bay, CA 82–84, 145
Balboni, Silvano 181–183
Balmat, Mary Adams 74–75, 98, *99*; see also Adams-Mastrovich Family Foundation
Bara, Lori 8, 16, 70, 105–107, *139*, 181, 183
Bara, Theda (screenwriter) 150
Baranger, François 5, 115
Baranger, Pauline Louise de Coppet 5
Bards of the Eisteddfod 93
Barrymore, Ethel 188, 199
Barrymore, John 188, 199
Barrymore, Lionel 103, 176, 187, 188, 199
Bartholomae, Phillip 125
Bat Mitzvah 9
Bathory, Elizabeth, Countess 130
Baton Rouge, Louisiana 36
Battle of Actium 83, 145
Battle of Mobile Bay 173, 175
Bava *151*, 152
Baxter, Warner 184, 197
Beast Garden, St Donat's Castle 94
Beast of the City 186–187, 198
Beaumont, Harry 190, 194
Beaumont, California 153
Beery, Wallace 184, 197
Bel-Air, California 107
Bel-Air Hotel 18
Belasco, David 166
Belasco Theater, New York City 109
Belgium 175
Bellamy, George 140
La Belle Russe 25, 81, *165*, 166, 196, 200
Ben-Hur 101, 181–183, 197
Bennett, Constance 62
Bennett, Joan 52, 62, 80
Benny, Jack 38, 67
Bentley 42

Index

Bergman, Ingrid 51, 52, 54, 56, 59, 61–64, 66, 75
Berle, Milton 103
Berlin, Irving 88
Berlin, Germany 147
Bern, Paul 187
Bernhardt, Sarah 12, 15, 16, 61, 124
Bernstein, Henri 187
Best Art Director, Academy Award, *Bridge Over San Luis Rey* 186
Best Color Cinematography, Academy Award, *Joan of Arc* 75
Best Color Costume Design, Academy Award, *Joan of Arc* 59
Best Supporting Actress, Academy Award, Hattie McDanie 187
Best Things in Life are Free 82
Beverly Hills, California 18, 25–26, 30, 32, 36, 60, 80, 96–97, 105
Beverly Hills Hotel 18, 55, 58
Beverly Hills Post Office 18
Beverly Hills Theater 75
Bickford, Charles 189, 199
Bijou Opera House, Milwaukee, WI 14
Biltmore Hotel, Los Angeles, CA 59, 60
Birchard, Robert, "Bob" 108
Bizet, George 123
Blache, Herbert 175
Blaine, Cecil 125
Blarney Castle 96
Blarney Stone 96
Blind Wives 196, 200
The Blue Flame 30, 111, *112*, 113, 168
Blue Ridge Mountains 179
Blythe, Betty 167
Board of Motion Picture Censors, Philadelphia, PA 124
Boardman, Eleanor 186, 198
Boleslawski, Richard 188
Bonaparte, Napoleon 142
Boone, Daniel 186
Borgia, Lucrezia 130
Boudrioz, Robert 180
Bowers, John 197
Brabin, Charles 21, *72*, 23, 32, 38, 42, 45–46, 52, 54, 56, 60–64, 67, 69, 78, 87–89, 92, 99, *100*, 101, 103–104, 106, 162, 164–166, 171, *172*, 173, 175, *177*, 178–189, 196–197, 199
Brabin, Susette Mosher 173, 178, 179
Brabout, Francesca *124*, 125
Bracken, Bertram 131, 132
Braddon, Mary 132
Bradenstoke Hall 94
Brady, Alice 188, 199
Brady, Phil 197
Brand, Cybil 38
Braufgam, Oto 173
Brazil diamond mines 184

Brenon, Herbert 58, 118, 121, 122, 164
Brentwood, CA (fire) 107
The Bridge of San Luis Rey 185, 198
Brighton Beach, NY 137
Brisson, Frederick 52, 62
Britain's official censor 118
Broadway, New York City 14, 52, 55, 62, 88, 109, 111, 114, 168, 185
The Broadway Peacock 180, 196
Brockwell, Gladys 184, 197
Bronx, New York 171, 175
Brooklyn critics 137
Broun, Heyward 112
Brower, Robert 173, 189–194
Brown, Captain Horace 92, 93
Brown, Mack 186 198
Brown, Martin 188
Brown Derby, Beverly Hills, CA 30, *31*
Bruno 64
Bucicault, Dion 162
Buckingham Palace 89, 91
Budai 38
Budd C-93 Conestoga 32
Buddha 42, *131*, 150, 152, 187,
Burnham, Julia 167
Burr, Aaron 6
Burr, Theodosia 6
Bushman, Francis Xavier 58, 135, 181, 183, 195, 197

Caesar 143
Calais, France 92
California 13, 17–19, 26, 30–31, 43, 48, 52, 59, 61–63, 70, 80–84, 88–89, 91, 96, 98–99, 103, 106–107, 110, 145–146, 152–153, 164, 183, 185–186, 189
California Here I Come 82
California Republican State Central Committee 88
Call Me Madam 88
Call of the Flesh 186, 198
Camille 142, *144*
Camille 143
Campbell Studios, New York City 15, 86
Canasta 73
Cape Florida 162
Capellani, Albert 175
Capitol Records 69
Captains Courageous 76
Carewe, Edwin 175
Carlisle, Archibald 132–133
Carlisle, Lady Isabelle 132, *133*
Carmen (character) 71, *123*, 124
Carmen (film) 70–71, 123–125, 128
Carmen (opera) 70, 123,
Caruso, Enrico 123
Catalina Island 186
Catholic Federation of Cincinnati 65

Index

Cavendish, Lady Charles 96; *see also* Astaire, Lady Charles Cavendish
Cavendish, Lord Charles Arthur Francis 96
CBS 127, 101
C.C. Brown's Ice Cream Parlor 48
Cecil, Bertie 134
Celebration of Purim 57
Chadwick Pictures 168
Chancellor of the Exchequer 93
Chaplin, Geraldine 70
Chertok, Jack 64
Chicago, Illinois 13, 116, 177, 179
A Child's Garden of Verses 171
Chimney Rock, Ashville, North Carolina 126
China 26, 28, 38, *74*, 105
Chorzele, Poland 5
Christian, King, X 65
Christians, Mady 189, 199
Christmas 42, 75, 108, 184
A Christmas Carol 173
Christmas Songs 69
Church of the Good Shepherd, Beverly Hills, CA 105
Churchill, Winston 92
Cigarettes *134*
Cincinnati, Ohio 5, 7–*10*, 12, 16, 65, 130
Claridge's Mayfair Hotel, London, England 91, 92
Clarke, Charles 38
Clary, Charles 38, 147, 197
The Claw 187
The Clemenceau Case 33, 118, *119*–120, 128
Cleopatra (film) 11, *40*, *45*–*46*, 54, 57–*58*, *82*, 83, *84*, 101, 143–144, *145*, 146, 182
Cleopatra (character) 11, *40*, 45, 46, 54, 83, *84*, *143*, 144, *145*, 146
Cleveland, Ohio 180
Clift, Montgomery 78, 80,
Coca, Imogene 103
The Colgate Comedy Hour 101
Collins, Dale 186
Collins, Daniel 175
Collins, John (pilot) 174
Collins, John (stage manager) 175
Collins, Richard 59
Columbia Records 69, 81
Commissary, Paramount Studios 78
Communism in Hollywood 59, 66, 69, 186
The Complete Andersen 65
Conner, Nadine 71
Cooper, Bigelow 189–191, 194, 199
Cooper, Miriam 44
Coronation of Queen Elizabeth II 89
Cosmopolitan Magazine 179

Cottonwood, Arizona 76
Coulter, John General 62
Coward, Noel 103
Craig, Betty *37*, *73*, *99*
Craig, James Reed 19
Craig, Joan 17, *18*–19, 22, *24*, 28, 37, *53*, 56, 63, *70*, *73*, *77*, *99*, *102*
Craig, John *19*, 28, 36, *37*
Craig Oil Company 17, *19*
Crain, Jeanne 38
Craven (Mobile Bay 1864) 173
Craven, Commodore Tunis Agustus MacDonough 174, 175
Creation's Tears 162
Cregar, Bess 74
Creger, Laird 74
Crews, Laura Hope 187, 199
Crystal ball 24, *27*, 28, 32
Culver City, California 183
Cummings, Robert 58
Cunobelinus, King 94
Cymbeline 94
Cyrano 62
Cyrano De Bergerac 62

Dagger 34, 123, 141, 159
La Dame aux Camelias 12, 142
Damita, Lili 185, 187, 198
Dance of the Seven Vails 153
Danneskjold, Nina (Nina Romano) 52, 61, 63–65
Danneskjold, Count Sophus 52, 61, 63, 64
D'Annunzio, Gabriele 120
The Darling of Paris 138
Daudet, Alphonse 131
Dauphin 62
David (Biblical) 42
Davidson, William B. *161*, 162, 195–196
Davidson Theatre, Milwaukee, WI 15
Davies, Marion 58, 92, 93, 95, 103
Davis, Bette 38, 103
Davis, Owen 111
Davis, William "Will" 125, 175
Dawley, James Searle 158, 172, 173
The Dawn of My Tomorrow 184
The Day Newspaper 136
Day of Reckoning 188–189, 199
Dayberth, Ida 8
Deadwood, North Dakota 73
de Broglie family 107
Decca Records 86
The Declaration of Independence, 173
de Coppet, Pauline Louise 5, 107
de Coppet, Régine (de Rininger) 5, 107
de Coppet, Theda 110
The Delicious Little Devil, 47
Delilah (Biblical) 130
DeMille, Cecil B. 124, 189
Desilu Studios 88

de Stael, Madame 107, 108
Destruction 125, 126
De Sylva, Buddy 52, 69, 81, 82, 85
Deutsches Theatre, Berlin 147
The Devil 109
The Devil's Daughter, 116, *120*, 128
Dexter, Elliott 184, 197
Dickens, Charles 178
Diehl, Penny 69
Disney, Roy 98
Disney, Walt *60*, 98
Disney "Main Street, USA" 98
Disneyland 98, 99
Dix, Richard 189
Dr. Jekyll and Mr. Hyde 76, 122
Dolan, Olga *166*, 167
Don Jose 123, 124
Doone, Mary *135*
Dos Pueblos Orchid Company 89, 91
Doty, Douglas Z. 168
Dove of Peace 42
Dover, England 92
Dover Shore cliffs, Newport Beach, CA 145
Driven (The Story of the Flock) 180–181, 196
Drummond, Else *137*
Du Barry *147*, 148, *149*
Du Barry, Madame (character) *147*, 148
Du Barry, Madame (novel) 147
Dublin, Ireland 96, 97
Dumond, Blanchette 156, *157*
Dunkelmyer and de Coppet Wig Makers 5, 10, 16
Dunne, Irene 188, 199
Duplessis, Marie 142
Dwan, Allen 65

East Lynne 132, *133*
Easter 54, 58, 59
Echo Park 45
Edendale Studios, Los Angeles, CA 45, 148
Edison, Thomas 171–172
Edison Company 164, 171–172, 190–194, 189
Edison Films 79, 172, 175, 179
Edison Studios 171, 172–173, 175, 177
Edison Trust 179
Edwards, J Gordon (director) 83, *126*, 134, 137, 140–143, 145, 147–148, 152, 154, 156, 158, 160, 162, 167, 184
Egan, Madam 76
Eiffel Tower 97
Egypt 35, 42, 47, 83, 116, 145
The Eisteddfod 93
Elizabeth II, Queen 89, 91–92
Elliott, Robert 162
Ellis Island 5

El Rancho Hotel, Las Vegas, NV 17
England 43, 55, 89–92, 97, 116, 134–135, 167, 173, 177, 181, 184
Erie, Pennsylvania 17
Erwin, Stuart 189
Esmeralda *138*, 139
Essanay Studios 179,194
Esther (Biblical) 9
Esther, Queen 57
The Eternal Sapho 131, *132*
Evans, Madge 186, 189, 198, 199
Exceptional Photoplays 180
An Exciting Day 10

Fagan, Myron C. 184
Fain, Sammy 38
Fair, Elinor 180, 196
Fairy Tales 65
Fairy with the Turquoise Hair 69
Falcon Crown 101
Farnum, Dorothy 186
Farnum, Marshall 121
Farrar, Geraldine 61, 111, 123–125
Father Knows Best 187
Father of the Bride 80
Fearnley, Jane 121, 164
Feldman, Charles K. 78
Ferber, Edna 184
Fernande 125
Ferrer, Jose 62, 63
Fireside Reminisces 172
Fireside Theater 101
First National Pictures 184, 197, 198
Fiske, Harrison Grey 109,110, 153
Fiske, Minnie Maddern 179, 194
Fitzroy, Emily 180, 196, 198
Fleming, Victor 51–56, 59, 61–64, 66–67, 75–76
Fleurette *25*, *165*, 166
Florida, St. Augustine 117, 141
The Flower of the Flock 179
Flying Tiger Line 30–131
A Fool There Was (film) 6, 94, 114–118, 128, 141
A Fool There Was (poem) 94
Footfalls 196, 200
Forbes, Ralph 185, 198
The Forbidden Path 148, *150*
Ford, Wallace 187, 198
Forest Lawn Memorial Park 106
The Formosa Cafe, 81
Fort Lee, New Jersey 30, 117, 123, 152, 157
Fort Tuthill, Arizona 68
45 Minutes from Hollywood 170
405 Freeway, CA 107
Fox, William 115, 122–123, 125, *139*, 152, 167
Fox Film Corporation 38, 136, 184, 128, 195, 196

Index 205

Fox Studios 117, 123, 125, 133, 135–136, 140, 152
Framed 184, 197
France 55–56, 92, 111, 122, 131, 134, *138*, 152, 155–156, 161, 173, 181, 185
Frankenstein 173, 178
Franklin, Benjamin 173
Franklin, Harry L. 175
French poodle 38
Freston, Herbert 60
Freston, Juanita 60
From Under My Hat 110
Fuller, Mary 164, 178, 189–192
Furness, Betty 189, 199

Gable, Clark 52–54, 62, 76, 101–102, 186, 198
Gabor, Eva 33
Gabor, Zsa Zsa 33
The Galley Slave *124*, 125
The Garden Theater, New York City 109
Gardner, Ava 38
Garland, Judy 80
Garmes, Lee 52, 54–55, 59
"Gateway to Kaintuck" 186
Gaudio, Tony 185
Gehry, Frank 99
Gelzer, Jay 179
Genghis Khan 187
Genie, magical 42
Genoa, Italy 181
"Gentlemen of Philadelphia" 74
George, Prime Minister David Lloyd 93
George VI, King 92
Georgia 122
Germany 36, 78, 96, 147, 158, 181
The Gettysburg Address 177
Ghost of the Talking Cricket 69
Gibbons, Cedric 186
Gilmore Stadium 60
La Gioconda *120*
Glamorgan, Wales 92
The Gleam 10
Glendale, California 106
The Globe Theatre 92
Glyn, Elinor 180
God Bless America 88
Godmother (Theda) 68, 148
Gold and the Woman 127, *128*
Goldilocks and the Three Bears 85
Goldwyn, Samuel 124, 181, 182
Goldwyn Pictures 180, 183, 196
Goleta, California 89
Gone with the Wind 52, 76, 185, 187
Goodman, Bernard 5
Goodman, Esther "Lori" 8
Goodman, Marque "Buddy" 8
Goodman, Mrs. 9
Goodman, Theda *8*

Goodman, Theo 10, 13
Goodman, Theodosia Burr 10
Goodrich, Frances 188
Gordin, Jacob 118, 163
Gordon, Ruth 111
Gorgeous George 67
Gramercy Park 96
Grand Opera House, Cincinnati, OH 12
Grauman, Sid 47, 48
Grauman's Chinese Theater 47
Grauman's Egyptian Theater 47
Great Depression 17
The Great Meadow 186, 198, 200
Great Moments with Lincoln 99
Great Seal of the Realm 97
Green Acres 103

Hackett, Albert 188
Haggard, Sir H. Rider 141
Hal Roach Studio 66
Hall, Ruth 52
Hall, Thurston 58
Haman (Book of Esther) 57
Hansel and Gretel 69
Hansen, Carl *87*
Hansen, Carroll Henderson *99*
Hard-Boiled Haggerty 184, 197
Hardy, Oliver 170
Harlequin 70
Harlow, Jean 187, 198
Harris, Marcia 163, 196
Harrison, Heather 55
Harrison, Kay 55, 59
Hathaway, Henry 38
Hazel 141
Healy, Ted 188, 199
Hearst, William Randolph 92–93, 95
Heart and Soul 141, *142*, *143*
Hecht, Ben 36
Hecht, Rose 47
Heidi 65
The Heiress 78, 80
Henried, Mimi 64
Henried, Monica 64
Henried, Paul 64
Henry, William 189, 199
Hepburn, Katharine 61
Her Double Life 134, *135*
Her Greatest Love 141
The Herald Tribune 159
Hersholt, Jean 64, 65, 187, 197–199
Heyes, Herbert 134, 137, *138*, 141
Hicks, Andi 108
Hilliard, Harry *128*, 141
Hilliard, Robert 114
Hilton, Nicky, Jr. 80
His First Commission 178
Hitchcock, Alfred Sir 55, 104
Hobart, George V. 111

Index

hole in the screen door 8
Hollywood 13, 18, 19, 31, 36, 47, 54, 57–61, 66, 74–76, 78–79, 81, 85, 88, 124, 168, 170, 175, 181, 183–184, 186–187; astrologer 54; blacklist 60, 186; celebrities 13, 38, 47, 54, 59, 63, 78; Communism 59; studio executives 66, 181
Hollywood Boulevard *31*, 57
Hollywood Ten 66
Holmby Hills, Los Angeles, CA 98
Holmes, Phillips 188, 199
Holmes, Stuart **124**, 125, **133**, **135**, 195, 198
Hoover, Pres. Herbert 186
Hoover Art Company, Los Angeles CA *13*
Hope 173
Hopkins, George James 145, 148, 153–154, 162
Hopper, DeWolf 110
Hopper, Hedda 110, 111
Hopper, Mason 175
Hotel Bel-Air, Los Angeles, CA 18
Hotel Plaza, New York City 184
House on Un-American Activities Committee (HUAC) 64
Hughes, Howard 187
Hugo, Victor 138
"hulky villain" 74
Hull, Thomas 17
human skeleton *35*
The Hunchback of Notre Dame 138
Hungary 109
Huntington Gardens 80
Huntington Library 80
Huston, Walter 186, 187, 198
Hutton, Betty 81

I Love Lucy 69
Illinois, Chicago 13, 116, 177, 179
I'm Dancing on a Rainbow 188
The Imperial Theater, Humboldt County, CA 185
Ince, John 175
Ince, Ralph W. 175
Ince, Thomas H. 180
Ireland 96–97, 164
Irena 189
Is the Right Little Girl for Me 188
Isaacs, Charles 26
Isabel Carlisle, Lady 132, **133**
Italy 55, 123, 136–137, 173, 181–183

Jack and the Beanstalk 70
Japan 18, 38, 140
Jarrico, Paul 59
Jean Hersholt Humanitarian Award 65
Jefferson, Thomas 173
Jesse L. Lasky Feature Play Company 124
Jesuit College of Sidney, Australia 172

Jesus (Biblical) 42
Jewish queen from Persia 9
Joan of Arc (character, person) 52, 56, 63–64, 66–67, 76
Joan of Arc (film) 54, 59, 61–62, 66, 75, 100
Joan of Lorraine 52, 54, 56, 59
Johnny Belinda 59
Johnson, Adrian 141–143, 147
Jolly Roger Restaurant 82
José, Edward 114
Josephus 153
Juliet 92, 127, **128**, 135, **136**
Juliet Cordova 127, **128**

Kanarek, Eliasz 24
Karloff, Boris 58, 102, 187, 199
Karma 45, 48, 85
Kathleen Mavourneen 162, **163**–164, 191, 196, 200
Kentucky 8, 180, 186
Kenyon, Charles 160
Kenyon, Doris 184–185, 197–198
Key, Kathleen 181, 183, 197
Kingston, Herbert Birch 180
Kingston, Natalie 184, 197
Kipling, Rudyard 94, 115, 116
Knollys, Carolyn **72**, **167**, 168
The Kreutzer Sonata, 118, 137

La Chaux-de-Fouds, Switzerland 5
The Lady 188
Lady Audley's Secret 121
The Lady from Philadelphia 10
Laguna Beach, California 81
La Jolla, California 26
Lake Arrowhead, California 63
Lanchester, Elsa 58, 103
Lansbury, Angela 58
Las Vegas Boulevard 17
Lasher, Matthew, Dr. 38
Lasky, Jesse 124, 125
Lasky Studios 124
La Tourette, Helen Craven 73
Laughton, Charles 58, 103
Law, Walter 138, 141, 143
Lawson, John Howard 186
Leiber, Fritz 143
Leimert, Lucille Cavanaugh 26, 27
Leimert, Walter 27
Liberty Theater, New York City 114
The Life of Lincoln, 99, 177
The Light 156–158
The Lights of New York, 180, 196, 200
Lillie 21
Lincoln, Abraham 99, 177, 178
Linden, Elmer 123
Lindstrom, Peter 62
Lismore Castle 96

Liverpool, England 177
Lloyd, Harold 103
Lloyd, Mildred 103
Lloyd George of Dwyfor 93
Lockhart, Gene 38
Lola 111
London, Jack 185
London, England 55, 91, 92, 97, 135, 184
The Lone Ranger 64
Long Beach, California 89, 146
Longfellow, Henry Wadsworth 171
Lord Byron 107
Los Angeles, California 13, 19, 26, 43, 52, 59, 63, 70, 91, 96, 98–99, 107, 110, 146, 189
Los Angeles Times 26, 56, 84, 181
Louis B. Mayer Pictures 183
Louisiana 36, 51, 157
Love and the Law 178
Loy, Myrna 187, 199
Lucas, Wilfred 175, 199
The Lure of Ambition **166**, 167
Luxembourg, (American Ambassador to) 87
Lynde, Mary 48, ***150***, 219
The Lyric Theater, New York City 143

Macbeth 94
MacMurray, Fred 38
Madame Mystereaux 169
Madame Mystery 169
Madonna and Child 34
Madrid, Spain 123
Magnin, Rabbi Edgar 105
Mandala 42
Marcus Welby, MD 187
Margie 38
marionettes 8, 9. 69
Mark Hopkins Hotel, San Francisco, CA 18
Masquers Club, Hollywood, CA 48
Martin, Florence 147, ***151***
Martin, Mary 141
Marx, Groucho 103
Marycrest Manor, Culver City, CA 107
The Mask of Fu Manchu, 102, 187, 199
Masquers Club, Hollywood, CA 48
Mata Hari 152
Mathis, June 181, 183
Max Factor 100
Maybelline 100
Mayer, Louis B. 100, 176, 183
McCardell, Roy L. 116
McConville, Bernard 116, 147
McDaniel, Hattie 187
McDermott, Marc 163–164, 172–173, 176, 178, 185, 189, 190–196, 198
McFarland, George "Spanky" 189, 199
McGlynn, Frank, Sr. 178, 193, 194

McIntyre, Cardinal James Francis 107
McKee, Raymond 163, 196
The Medal and the Maid 177
Medusa 122, 130
mellow drama 14
Menjou, Adolphe 38, 59, 60, 63
Mercer, Johnny 81
Merimee, Prosper 124
Merkel, Una 188, 189,199
Merman, Ethel 88
Merwin, Bannister 173
Mesta, George 87
Mesta, Perle **87**
Metro-Goldwyn-Mayer (MGM) 197–199
Metro Pictures 135, 175, 183, 196
Metropolitan Opera, New York City 70, 123, 185
Mexican Revolution 34, 123, 185–189
MGM Studios 50, 66, 80, 183, 195
Miami Beach Casino 162
Mills, Albert 16
Milwaukee, Wisconsin 13, 14, 16
The Milwaukee Sentinel 130
Minnelli, Liza **70**
Minnelli, Vincente 80
Miracle Mile District, Los Angeles, CA 20
Miracle on 34th Street 38
Mismates 184, 197
Miss Blue 23, 35, 51, 101, 103
Molnar, Ferenc 109
Monte Carlo Casino 140
Moore, Colleen 184, 197
Morley, Karen 187, 199
Morley, Victor 110
Moses (Biblical) 42
Mosher, Sam 31, 89, 91
Mosher, Susette 173, 178, 179
Moths 141
Motion Picture Alliance for the Preservation of American Ideals 59
Motion Picture Association of America 59
Motion Pictures Patents Company (MPPC) 177, 179
Mound Street Temple, Cincinnati, Ohio 9
Murillo, Mary 131, 132
Murphy, George 88
Murray, Ken 103
Murray, Mae 46, 47, 58, 70, 93, 111
Mussolini, Benito 181–182
My Favorite Martian 64

Naish, J. Carroll 199
The National Board of Review of Motion Pictures 153
The National Committee for Better Films 180
National Legion of Decency 65
NBC 101

Neely, Hugh Munro 108
Nesbitt, Miriam 173, 189–194
The *Nevada Daily Mail* 136
Newbolt, Sir Henry 174
New Jersey 30–32, 36, 54, 79, 117, 152, 157, 172
New Morals for Old 187, 199
New Orleans, Louisiana 51, 157
New South Wales 172
New York City 6, 12, 13, 15, 30, 52, 54, 57, 59, 62–63, 66, 79, 86, 96, 99, 114, 123, 130, 133, 143, 148, 152, 159, 167, 176, 179–180, 184, 192, 196, 200
New York Library for the Performing Arts 7, 41
New York Public Library 139
New York Times 80, 109, 111, 175
New York Wire 56
Newport Bay (Upper) 82, 84, 145
Newport Beach 84, 145
The Newport News 84
Nibbles and Me 80
Niblo, Fred 182, 183
Nilsson, Anna Q. 185, 198
Nixon, Richard 64
Nixon, Mrs. Richard 64
North Carolina 126
North Dakota 73
North Shore Tavern 63, 64
Nova Scotia 96, 178, 179
Novarro, Ramon 182, 183, 186, 197, 198
Nubian slaves 83, 184
Nye, G. Raymond 153, *158*

O'Brien, Margaret 85
Ocean House 103
Ochs, Weihl and Goodman, Tailors 5, 10
Octavian 83
O'Day, Molly 184, 197
Ogle, Charles 173, 176, 178, 189 -193
O'Hara, Maureen 38
O'Hara, Scarlett 185
Ohio 5, 7–12, 16, 35, 65, 122, 130, 180
Oklahoma City, Oklahoma 87
Oland, Warner 122, 197
Old Testament days 9
158th Infantry Regiment *68*, 69, 148
Oppenheim, James 173
Ordeal 186
Oregon, Portland 110
Oscar 59, 185, 186, 187
O'Sullivan, Maureen 58, 103, 188, 199
Ouida 134, 141
Ouija Board 101

Pabst Theater, Milwaukee, WI 14, 16
Page, Brett 156
Pageant of the Masters, Laguna Beach, CA 81

Palace Hotel, San Francisco, CA 18
Palm Garden Schlitz Hotel, Milwaukee, WI *13*
Pantages Theater, Hollywood, CA 187
Paramount Studios 78, 80, 81
Paris, France 55, 92, 97, 111, 122, 131, *138*, 152, 156, 161, 185
Parker, Jean 189, 199
Parks, Larry 58, 67
Parsons, Louella 116
Pasadena, California 30, 80
Pathé Films 114
Payton, Ann 51–53, *99*, 103
Payton, Claude 162
Payton, Hayes 36, 51–*53*, 103
peacock dress 57, *58*
Pearl Harbor, Hawaii 68
Pearson, Virginia 114, 195
Peck, Gregory 48
Pennsylvania 10, 17, 32, 52, 74, 124
Pennsylvania Board of Motion Picture Censors 124
Perry, Margaret 187, 199
Persia 9, 11
The Personal Recollections of Joan of Arc 56
Peru 64, 185
Peter Pan 24, *25*
Petrovitch, Princess *140*
Philadelphia, Pennsylvania 10, 74, 124
Philbin, Mary 184, 197
Philipson, David, Rabbi 9
Phillips, August 164, 173, 189–193
Phoenix Junior College 68
Pickfair 103
Pickford, Mary 75, 103, 148, 184
Pierce Brothers Mortuary, Beverly Hills, CA 105
Pinocchio 69, 70
The Pittsburg Press 118
A Place in the Sun 78, 80
Plaza Hotel (New York) 184
Plunkett, Walter 185
Poe, Edgar Allan 94, 95, 171, 179
Poland, Chorzele 5
Polito, Sol 184, 185
Polynesian restaurant, Beverly Hills, CA 32
Ponds Cream 100
Poppea 154
Popular Magazine 178
Porter, Edwin S. 172, 178
Portland, Oregon 110
Powell, Frank 114–116, 129
Prescott, Robert "Bob" 30–32, 38
SS *President Roosevelt* 89
The Promised Land (Biblical) 42, 186
Puchta, George (mayor of Cincinnati, OH) 130

Puddy 34, 101
Punch and Judy 70
Pung Chow *74*
puppets 9, 70, 69

The Quaker Girl 110
Queen Esther (Biblical) 57
Queen of Egypt 145
Queen of the Nile *45*
Queen's Beasts 90

Rasputin and the Empress 176, 188, 199
Raven *93*, 179
The Raven (photoplay) 179, 194, 200
The Raven (poem) 94, 200
Reagan, Ronald 38, 59, 64, 88
"Red" (Joan Craig) 22, 160
Red Cross Seal Story 173, 190
Red River 78
Reed, Florence 111
Reed, Luther 156
Reid, Wallace 124
Reno, Nevada 17
Righter, Carroll 52, 54, 62
Roach, Hal 168–170
Robards, Jason, Sr. 184, 197
Roberts, Elizabeth M. 186
Robinson, Edward G. 58
Rockwell, Norman 81
Rocky Point 83, 84; *see also* Balboa Island, Newport Bay, CA
Rodolfo, Signor 47; *see also* Valentino, Rudolf
Romano, Nina 52, 61; *see also* Danneskjold, Nina; Tellegen, Nina
Rome, Italy 55, 181
Romeo 136, 159
Romeo and Juliet 92, 94, 135, *136*, 137
Rosa 122
Roscoe, Alan 153, 162
Roscoe, Albert 45, 143, *151*, 154, 156
The Rose of Blood 90, *146*, 147
Rossellini, Roberto 75
Roswell, New Mexico 64
Royal Mews (Buckingham Palace) 91
Russell, Rosalind 52, 54, 62

St Alban's Church, Westwood, CA 76
St. Augustine, Florida 117, 141
St. Donat's Castle, Glamorgan, Wales 92–95
St. Francis Hotel, San Francisco, CA 18
St. Francis Xavier's College, Liverpool, England 177
St. Monica's Catholic Church, Santa Monica, CA 106
St. Petersburg Times 116
Saks Fifth Avenue 71
Salem, New Jersey 54

Salome 2, *27*, 152–*153*
San Bernardino, California 152
San Fernando Valley, California 61
San Francisco, California 18, 164, 185
Santa Barbara, California 91
Santa Monica, California 48, 62, 103, 106
Santa Monica Mountains, California 62
Sapho 131
Sarony *62*
"Satanic Sorceress of the Screen" 121
Savage, Henry W. 109–110
Schallert, Edwin 56
Schellinger, Rial 131
Schenck, Joe 44
Schleswig, Madame 110
Schlitz Hotel, Milwaukee, WS 13, 14
Schlitz Palm Garden *13*
Schlitz Uihlein Alhambra Theater, Milwaukee, WS 14
The Schubert Theater, NYC 111–113, 168
Screen Actors Guild (SAG) 59, 64, 88
Sealyham 18
The Search 78
Sears, Zelda 189, 199
The Secret of Madame Blanche 188, 199
Selwyn, Ruth 187, 199
Selznick, Lewis 111
September Song 63
Sequoia National Park 185
The Serpent 41, 65, 125, *127*
"Serpent of the Nile" 143
702 North Alpine Drive *28*
Seville, Spain 123, 126, 156
Shakespeare, William 36, 92, 94, 135–136, *136*
Shakespeare of Hollywood 36
The She-Devil 49, 154, *155*
Shearer, Norma 103
Sherman Antitrust Act 179
The Ship from Shanghai 186, 198
Shrine Auditorium, Los Angeles, CA 70
Sierra Pictures 56, 63
Signal Oil and Gas Company 31
Sills, Milton 184, 185, 197–198
Sin 122, 128
The Siren's Song 160
Six Days 180, 181, 196
649 West Adams Blvd 43, *44*
skeleton *see* human skeleton
Skirvin, Bill 87
Skirvin Towers Hotel, Oklahoma City, OK 87
So Big 184, 197
Solt, Andrew P. 56, 64
Song of Russia 59
Songwriter's Hall of Fame 82
The Soul of Buddha 43, 150, *151*, 152
Southampton, England 89
Spain 123, 155–156

Sphinx 38, *40*, 116
Sporting Blood 101–102, 186, 189, 198, 200
Spreckels, Adolph, II 18, 52
Spreckels, Kay 52, 54
Stage Mother 188, 199
The Stain 114
Standard & Poor's Blue Book 85
Standing, Wyndham 168
Star of David (Biblical) 42
Starrett, Charles 187
Statement Magazine 108
Stella Maris 184, 197, 200
Steuart, Eldean 113
Steuart, Loel 113
Stevens, George 78
Stevens, Louis 185–186
Stevenson, Robert Louis 171
stock market 85
Stone, Lewis 187, 199
The Story of the Flock (Driven) 180
The Strike at the Mines 178
Sunny Side Up 82
Sunset Boulevard, Beverly Hills, CA 18
"Super Deluxe Screen Format" 138, 140
Sutton, George W., Jr 184
"The Sweetest Day of the Year" 180
Swickard, Josef 153
Switzerland 5
Sydney, Australia 172

Tableau Vivant 8, 165
Tackaberry, John 38, 67
Talmadge, Norma 38, 44, 48, 111
Taylor, Elizabeth 80
Taylor, Robert 59, 199
Teal, Conway 189
Technicolor 53, 55, 56, 88
USS *Tecumseh* 174, 175
Teddy (Theda) 8, 9, 115
Tellegen, Lou 61, 124
Tellegen, Nina 61
Tellegen, Rex 61, 66
Temple, Shirley 65
Ten Commandments (Biblical) 42
Terry, Ellen 94
Thalberg, Irving 188
Thar's a Nice Girl 188
Theda Bara, I'll Keep Away from You *129*
There's No Business Like Show Business 88
Thomas, J. Parnell 64
Thomas, Sir 93
The Three Jewels (Buddhist) 42
Three Wise Men (Biblical) 42
Throne Room (Buckingham Palace) 81
The Tiger Woman *140*
Tillers of the Soil 180
Timeline Films 108
Tolstoy, Leo 118

Tone, Franchot 188, 199
Tony Award(s) 59, 62
Tooker, William H. 133, 195
Torrence, Ernest 185, 186, 198. 199
Toscanini, Arturo 123
Tour d'Argent 97
Tracy, Spencer 58, 80
La Traviata 142
Truman, Pres. Harry 87
Tudor style mansion 43
Tusing, Anna 8
Twain, Mark 56, 171
Twinkletoes 184, 197
Two Orphans *121*, 122

The Unchastened Woman *72*, *167*, 168
Under the Yoke *151*, 152
Under Two Flags *134*
Underwood and Underwood Studios, NYC 6, *79*
University of California at Berkeley, CA 173
University of Cincinnati 10
The Usurer's Grip 178, 189

Valentino, Rudolph 47
The Valley of the Giants 185, 197
Valverda, Maria *151*, 152
"Vamp" 4, 8, *35*, 85, 103, 105, 111, 116–117, 128, 134–135, 164
Vampire 94, 111, 115–117, 122, 128–130, 137
The Vampire (poem) 94, 115, 116
Vance, Leta Nicholson 111
Vanderbilt(s) 12
Van Druten, John 187
Vania 125, *127*
Vanity Fair 179, 194
Velasquez, Edward 123
Verona, Italy 136, 137
Victorian architecture 8, 13
Vidor, King 58
Villa, Gen. Pancho 34, 123, 134, 159
villain 70
Vincent, James 127
Vincent, Ruth 177
Vitaphone 185
The Vixen *137*

Waldorf-Astoria Hotel (New York) 59, 66
Wales, Glamorgan 92
Wallace, Vice Pres. Henry 61
Wallich, Glenn 81
Wallich's Music City 85
Walnut Hills High School 9
Walsh, Raoul 44, 58, 71, 123, 125–126, 181
Walt Disney Concert Hall 99
Walthall, Henry B. 179, 185, 194, 198

Walton, Douglas 188, 198
Wanger, Walter 52, 54–56, 62–63, 66, 75
Warner, Jack L. 60
Warner Brothers 60, 180, 185
Washington (state) 110
Washington Masquerade 187, 199
We Look and See 171
Welsh festival 93; *see also* The Eisteddfod
West Adams Boulevard 42–*44*
West Coast 18
Western Costume Company 57
Western Union Telex 63
Westlake School for Girls *77*
Westminster Abby 90
Westwood, California 76
Westwood Village, Los Angeles, CA 76, 106, 107
What Happened to Mary 178, 189
Wheatcroft, Stanhope 133
When a Woman Sins 153, *154*
When Men Desire *12*, *158*–160
While New York Sleeps 179, 196, 200
White, Glen 138, 141, 143
White, Pearl 180, 196
White Drawing Room (Buckingham Palace) 192
Whitney, Claire 125, 133, 141
Wilder, Thornton 185
Willard, John 111
Wilshire and Highland station 20

Wilshire Boulevard 20
Wing and a Prayer 38
Wisconsin, Milwaukee 13–14, 16
Witch with a Broom 69
The Wizard of Oz 76
The Wolf's Claw 125
Wolheim, Louis 186, 195, 198
A Woman There Was *161*, 162
The Woman with the Hungry Eyes 108
Women's Improvement Club of Cincinnati 9
Woodward, Eugenie 133
Woolworth Tower, New York City 178
World War I 184, 188
World War II 27. 38, 78
World's Fair 1964 (New York) 99
Wyman, Jane 49, 59

The Yearling 48
"yin-yang" 42
Yosemite 185
Yost, Herbert 178, 191–192
Young, Robert 187, 199
Yucaipa, California 153
Yusupov, Felix, Prince 188

Zanol Lorens La Bara 16
Zara *161*, 162
Zola, Emile 125